D0064984

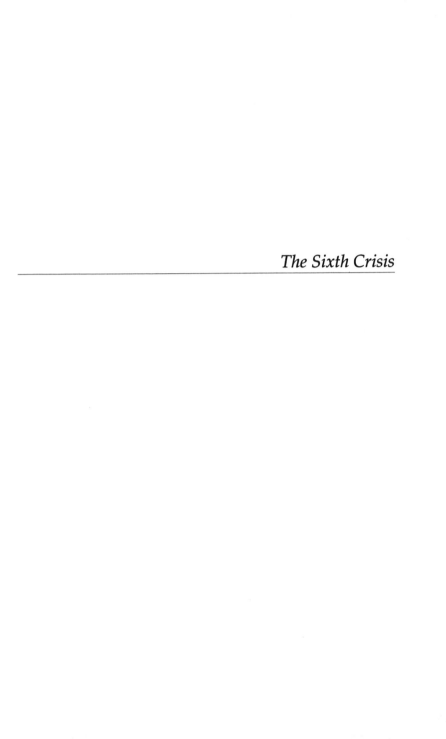

The Sixth Crisis

DANA H. ALLIN AND
STEVEN SIMON

The Sixth Crisis

Iran, Israel, America and the Rumors of War

OXFORD
UNIVERSITY PRESS

2010

 IISS An International Institute for Strategic Studies book

OXFORD
UNIVERSITY PRESS

Oxford University Press, Inc., publishes works that further
Oxford University's objective of excellence
in research, scholarship, and education.

Oxford   New York
Auckland   Cape Town   Dar es Salaam   Hong Kong   Karachi
Kuala Lumpur   Madrid   Melbourne   Mexico City   Nairobi
New Delhi   Shanghai   Taipei   Toronto

With offices in
Argentina   Austria   Brazil   Chile   Czech Republic   France   Greece
Guatemala   Hungary   Italy   Japan   Poland   Portugal   Singapore
South Korea   Switzerland   Thailand   Turkey   Ukraine   Vietnam

Published by Oxford University Press, Inc.
198 Madison Avenue, New York, New York 10016

www.oup.com

Oxford is a registered trademark of Oxford University Press

Library of Congress Cataloging-in-Publication Data
Allin, Dana H., 1958–
The sixth crisis : Iran, Israel, America, and the rumors of war / Dana H. Allin and
Steven Simon.
p. cm.
Includes bibliographical references and index.
ISBN 978–0–19–975449–6
1. Nuclear weapons—Iran.   2. Iran—Military policy.   3. Israel—Military policy.
4. Iran—Foreign relations—United States.   5. United States—Foreign
relations—Iran.   6. Iran—Foreign relations—Israel.   7. Israel—Foreign
relations—Iran.   I. Simon, Steven.   II. Title.
UA853.I7A45 2010
355.02′170955—dc22   2010014504

9 8 7 6 5 4 3 2 1

Printed in the United States of America
on acid-free paper

For my father, Julius Simon

———

For my daughter, Sophie

And you will hear of wars and rumors of wars;
See that you are not alarmed; for this must take
place, but the end is not yet

—Matthew 24:7 (RSV)

Acknowledgments

This book is the product of the authors' mutual and separate interests and preoccupations going back for years. Convinced that U.S. foreign policy, particularly regarding the Middle East, went fundamentally off the rails in the years after September 11, 2001, we were both hopeful about the Obama administration's efforts to get America back on track, and apprehensive about its chances of success. The build-up of tensions stemming from Iran's progress toward a nuclear capability, along with the tragic and dangerous stalemate between Israel and Palestine, seemed to us to call out for a book-length assessment of Obama strategies and Middle East realities.

A principal vehicle for our inquiry has been a series of International Institute for Strategic Studies (IISS) workshops assessing the Iranian challenge in relation to the wider array of Middle East conflicts and tensions. The project was supported generously by the Carnegie Corporation of New York; we are grateful to the Corporation and to its tireless Stephen Del Rosso for this support. The IISS provided an excellent base for this project as well as a long-term intellectual home for Dana Allin, and for this we are indebted to many IISS colleagues, including John Chipman, IISS Director-General; Adam Ward, Director of Studies; Mark Fitzpatrick, Co-director of the Iran project; and Jeffrey Mazo, Managing Editor of *Survival*.

Portions of chapters 1, 2, and 5 are adapted from previous publications: Dana H. Allin and Steven Simon, "Military Force Will Not Defeat Islamist Revivalism," *Financial Times* (October 9, 2006); Steven Simon, "An Israeli Strike on Iran," CPA Contingency Planning Memorandum No.5 (The Council on Foreign Relations, November 2009); Dana H. Allin and Steven Simon, "The Moral Psychology of U.S. Support for Israel," *Survival*, 45, 3 (Autumn 2003); and Dana H. Allin, "The United States: The Primacy of Politics," *Strategic Survey 2009: The Annual Review of World Affairs* (London: Routledge for IISS, 2009). Permission to republish this material is gratefully acknowledged.

The final research and actual writing of this book against a very tight deadline would have been impossible without the prodigious research support of Dina Esfandiary and Rachel Segal of IISS, to whom no expression of gratitude can be adequate, and Ed Stein of CFR, who helped tremendously despite his other commitments. Crucial support at earlier stages was provided by Matthew Harries, Sara Moeller, Sarah Hexter, and Ben Rhode.

A number of colleagues have reviewed chapters or the whole manuscript at various stages, or offered analytical guidance on specific questions; we thank Ali Ansari, Aluf Benn, James Dobbins, Toby Dodge, Mark Fitzpatrick, Gregory Gause, Erik Jones, Ariel Levite, David Makovsky, Robert Malley, Jeffrey Mazo, Steven Miller, Nader

Mousavizadeh, Alan Richards, Ben Rhode, Ray Takeyh, Adam Ward, and Carolyn West for their thoughtful comments. They will not all agree with our conclusions, but they deepened our understanding greatly. Errors of fact or interpretation are, of course, ours alone.

Our editor at Oxford University Press, David McBride, gave wise advice and a scrupulous eye to the shaping of the manuscript, while Oxford's Alexandra Dauler, Jessica Ryan, and Marc Schneider helped us navigate the production process.

Finally, this book would hardly have been possible without the love and forbearance of our immediate family members: Elisabeth, Christoph, and Sophie—on one side of the ocean—and Virginia on the other. Their support is always generous, but this time the magnitude and urgency of the stakes made us appreciate even more that they are our truest and most cherished collaborators.

Contents

Introduction

THE INAUGURATION OF PRESIDENT BARACK OBAMA, witnessed under a cold, clear sky by the largest crowd ever to converge on Washington, was an event of profound historical fulfillment. Yet the new president marked the occasion with a speech that was sober, prosaic, and grim. His peroration featured words that the most stolid of American heroes, George Washington, ordered to be read out in 1776 on the brink of defeat: "Let it be told to the future world...that in the depth of winter, when nothing but hope and virtue could survive...that the city and the country, alarmed at one common danger, came forth to meet [it]." Obama made his comparison to "this winter of our hardship," 232 years later, explicit.

The "gathering clouds" of which the president also spoke included financial and economic meltdown, endless war in Afghanistan, and potentially catastrophic climate change. "You never want a serious crisis to go to waste," said Rahm Emanuel, the designated White House chief of staff, a few weeks after Obama's election. He went on to explain: "things that we had postponed for too long, that were long-term, are now immediate and must be dealt with."[1] Emanuel was talking mainly about domestic troubles, regarding which Obama in his first year and a half as president has had some successes—notably on health-care reform—and other disappointments. Foreign policy, where the Obama agenda is equally ambitious, may prove even more difficult. In particular, the United States remains mired in the Greater Middle East, with much responsibility but less in the way of solutions to the region's stubborn conflicts.

Since World War II, Washington has confronted five distinct crises, each drawing America progressively deeper into the Middle East. Some have been handled skillfully, while at least one was mishandled catastrophically, but in no case were the underlying problems resolved. Each crisis has had lasting deleterious effects and has reshaped the Middle East and America's role in it, while compounding the difficulty of the next crisis.[2]

In 1956, the bizarre plot by Britain, France, and Israel to retake the Suez Canal, and perhaps topple Nasser in the process, convinced U.S. president Dwight D. Eisenhower that he had to protect America's reputation from the blowback of Arab anticolonial anger. His decision had the effect of aborting the plot and humiliating America's allies, without, however, achieving any notable success in stemming Arab radicalism. In the extended crisis of 1967–1973—seven years that were bracketed by two Arab-Israeli wars—the United States in effect took ownership of the conflict, sided more overtly and more or less permanently with Israel, weathered a brief oil embargo that intensified an ongoing energy price shock, and confronted the Soviet Union with a nuclear alert. Emerging from the crisis some months after the second of those wars, Washington had established, not least through Henry Kissinger's bravura diplomacy, its strategic and diplomatic preeminence in the region, but it had also become fatefully associated with Israel's occupation of Palestinian territories. In 1979, an Islamic revolution convulsed Iran and toppled a key American ally, sent tremors of fear through Arab regimes, precipitated an almost decadelong war with Iraq, and helped ruin an American presidency. America's unsteady adjustment to the new political force of radical Islam unfolded over the next several years of hostage taking, the assassination of Anwar Sadat, and the suicide bombings that killed hundreds of American and French military personnel in their barracks in Beirut as well as destroying the U.S. embassy and killing 63 people six months earlier. In 1990, Iraqi forces under Saddam Hussein invaded Kuwait. The United States led successful diplomacy and a triumphant land war to eject them, but then found itself in an exhausting 20-year strategic embrace of Iraq—first containment, then invasion and occupation—with bitter consequences that continue today. On September 11, 2001, the United States suffered the worst attack on its homeland since the War of 1812, with nearly 3,000 horrific deaths. This crowning act of Sunni terrorist extremism pulled the United States into a lengthy war in Afghanistan, an ill-conceived invasion of Iraq, and an assault on its own constitutional principles at home.

When Obama took the oath of office on January 20, 2009, he inherited these accumulated traumas. And the United States was now confronting a sixth Middle East crisis, with perhaps the greatest potential to undo

Obama's ambitions abroad, wreck his domestic plans at home, and destroy his presidency. Iran is developing a nuclear weapons capability. There is every reason to worry that, in the coming years or even months, a fearful Israel will conclude that it is cornered, with no choice but to launch a preventive war aimed at crippling Tehran's nuclear infrastructure and thereby removing—or at least forestalling—what most Israelis consider a threat to the Jewish state's very existence.

The Israeli calculations are not crazy. Iran's regime is once again puffing itself up as the avatar of Islamic radicalism, drawing on the Muslim world's anger and hatred of Israel. The state coup that attended the disputed elections of June 12, 2009, has had the effect of consolidating power around a Supreme Leader who has described Israel as a "cancerous tumor" that must be "removed from the region," and a president who has called Israel a "dried up and rotten tree which will be annihilated with one storm."[3] This is the same leadership that funnels money and weapons to Hamas and Hezbollah terrorists for the purpose of killing Israeli Jews. Israelis thus see weapons of nuclear annihilation serving an annihilationist agenda, and in the long shadow of the *Shoah* they have little patience for those who parse the Iranian statements in terms of *political* rather than physical destruction. The chasm under inaction is death—such is not an unreasonable way for Jews to read their own history. Conversely, when Israel acted in the past, it was usually happy with the results. In 1981, Israeli planes destroyed the Iraqi reactor at Osirak—to loud international condemnation, and quiet international relief. In 2007, the Israelis destroyed a nuclear facility in Syria; this time even the Syrians kept quiet. To do what needs to be done, and then ride out the reaction, can seem a reasonable approach in a hostile world.

But it can also breed hubris. For the Israeli panic, which runs along the well-worn grooves of Israelis' mentality of siege, is straining the one thing that Israel's governments for a more than a generation have relied on: a special relationship with the United States based on American empathy for Israel as a like-minded democracy. Obama's America is not, of course, completely transformed, but it is moving in a different direction. Chastened by its misadventure in Iraq, it is looking for another way beyond shock and awe to cope with the problem of Muslim rage on a global scale. With the liberal ascendancy in Washington, the new administration wants to recast relations. It has shifted policy toward the Israel—Palestine impasse in subtle but significant ways, with a much clearer determination that Israel's occupation of Palestinian territory and expansion of settlements is a threat both to Israeli democracy's long-term viability and to America's broader interests in the region, including a gradual cutoff in the supply of recruits to terrorism. And the Obama administration is concerned, with good reason, that air strikes against Iran's nuclear facilities might not be a limited affair: in the worst case, they could ignite a general war between Israel and Iran that would suck in the United States; drive millions of Arabs, Sunnis, as well as Shi'a, to side with Iran; reinvigorate the terrorist jihad; destroy the Israel-Palestine peace process; and decisively end America's attempt to restore its moral footing and reestablish its leadership role in the world. And the painful irony is that they would probably not stop Iran from developing nuclear weapons anyway. The program might be set back by a couple of years, but Iran could redouble its efforts and very likely succeed in circumstances far more fragile than we already face.

This discussion, of course, continued against the backdrop of the moving and terrible scenes of protest and repression on the streets of Tehran and other cities after Iran's apparently fraudulent June 12 elections. This drama has deepened the crisis in two ways. First, it compounds the paralysis of Iranian decision making and at the same time turns American engagement with Tehran into a more complicated moral enterprise. Second, the elections drama reminds many thoughtful Israelis that an Israeli attack would—in the words of one Tel Aviv professor—open up "an historical account" between the Jewish state and the Iranian people that might be difficult ever to close.[4]

This spiral of disaster could feed back into American domestic politics as well. After his first year in office, Obama was still reasonably popular but also potentially vulnerable to familiar right-wing accusations of appeasement. Israel does not want a rupture with the United States, but Obama can probably not afford a rupture with Israel. The Israel-Iran war would not only bring us into renewed conflict with Muslims, it would reignite the domestic battle over the war on terror, which has been further poisoned in the debate over torture. Although it may seem improbable, foreign policy disaster could make Obama a one-term president. His replacement by a right-wing Republican would end this moment of liberal optimism, just as it would overturn hopes for a rapprochement with the Muslim world.

In the eight months from November 2008, America, Israel, and Iran each held elections. The most dramatic expectations of change were invested in the United States. For America's position in the world this carries a certain irony, since the Obama approach to foreign affairs is, in many respects, a fundamentally conservative one. His advisers took charge of U.S. foreign policy as self-declared "realists." For Democratic foreign policy elites in general, this explicit new branding followed naturally from the general repudiation of the Bush administration's neoconservative idealism. During the election campaign, Senator Obama had frequently cited the foreign policies of the first Bush administration as a model worthy of emulation, pointing specifically to the axis of realists among the elder Bush's advisers, including Brent Scowcroft, James Baker, and Colin Powell.

The word *realism* can be no more than a slogan, of course, and an implicit claim that one's views are realistic and one's opponent's are not. It refers to a specific school and theory of international relations, but that theory transfers only partially and imperfectly to the realm of real politics and strategy. The word's fuzziness is demonstrated by the fact that it can be used to support a greater emphasis on hard military power or a greater emphasis on diplomatic accommodation. Obama's emphasis was the latter, and the approach opened him up to two general allegations: first, that his administration was ready to sacrifice basic values, as when Secretary of State Hillary Clinton traveled to China and subordinated the problem of human rights to necessary strategic cooperation with Beijing; and second, that his overtures to antagonists such as Iran were naive because they were unlikely to be reciprocated.

But Obama in his campaign rhetoric and the first 16 months of his presidency demonstrated a somewhat different aspect of foreign policy realism that might best be described as *psychological realism*, an intuitive understanding that the United States was unable to impose its own moral and historical narrative on the rest of the world. This may seem obvious enough, yet it has been surprisingly difficult for American leaders to address the rest of the world or their own citizens in a way that does not convey an assumption of moral superiority or hubristic "exceptionalism." On one of his first trips abroad, speaking in a press conference following the April 2008 NATO summit in Strasbourg, Obama was asked whether he actually believed in the concept of American exceptionalism. The president replied:

> I believe in American exceptionalism, just as I suspect that the Brits believe in British exceptionalism and the Greeks believe in Greek exceptionalism. I'm enormously proud of my country and its role and history in the world. If you think about the site of this summit and what it means, I don't think America should be embarrassed to see evidence of the sacrifices of our troops, the enormous amount of resources that were put into Europe postwar, and our leadership in crafting an Alliance that ultimately led to the unification of Europe. We should take great pride in that. And if you think of our current situation, the United States remains the largest economy in the world. We have unmatched military capability. And I think that we have a core set of values that are enshrined in our Constitution, in our body of law, in our democratic practices, in our belief in free speech and equality, that, though imperfect, are exceptional. Now, the fact that I am very proud of my country and I think that we've got a whole lot to offer the world does not lessen my interest in recognizing the value and wonderful qualities of other countries, or recognizing that we're not always going to be right, or that other people may have good ideas, or that in order for us to work collectively, all parties have to compromise and that includes us.[5]

Such commonsensical remarks were enough to ignite a scandal among neoconservative and other right-wing commentators, who accused him of using almost every foreign trip as occasion for an extended "apology tour."[6]

This was a ridiculous charge. Any fair reading of Barack Obama's writings and statements show him to be an authentic American nationalist who is unabashedly proud of the American narrative. He is simply not so deluded as to imagine the United States can make understanding and cooperation with the rest of the world dependent on the whole world sharing that distinct American understanding of its own historical significance.

The president's psychological realism came through most clearly in his June 4, 2009, speech, delivered in Cairo and addressed to the Muslim communities of the world. The speech was striking for the president's obvious determination to speak to his audience like adults. It was time, said Obama, to "say in public what we say in private" and to "act on what everyone knows to be true."[7] The Obama administration had started on that plan by demanding, without loopholes or equivocation or codicils, that Israel finally stop its expansion of settlements in the occupied territories.

This demand set up a surprisingly early confrontation with Israel's new coalition government under Benjamin Netanyahu, who had become prime minister for the second time after his Likud party came in a close second to the governing Kadima bloc in the February 2009 elections, but was able to form a right-wing coalition after Kadima failed to form a government. The Israelis claimed that the U.S. administration was reneging on an oral agreement that had been reached with the Bush White House, under which U.S. opposition to settlement construction would allow for the exception of "natural growth" to existing settlements. Obama officials said they knew nothing of such an unwritten understanding and, in any event, the recurring spectacle of new Israeli buildings was understandably corrosive to Palestinian confidence that the Israelis would ever contemplate giving the territories back in a negotiated settlement.

The Israelis seemed genuinely puzzled that the new administration was taking the settlements issue so seriously. On May 18, during his first visit to Washington after becoming prime minister, Netanyahu pressed his case that the far more urgent problem was dealing with Iran's nuclear program. Only after the existential threat was removed could Israel contemplate serious further concessions to the Palestinians for the purpose of a final peace agreement. At a joint press conference following their White House meeting, Obama contradicted his Israeli guest rather sharply: if there was a linkage between the two issues, the president argued, it went in the other direction; progress on the Israel—Palestine front was needed in order to enlist Arab support for a strategy of containing and pressuring Iran.

On the face of it, Obama, the supposed pragmatist, was taking a rather bold gamble by staking so much of his prestige on a settlement of both the Israel-Palestine conflict and the Iranian nuclear crisis. In particular, Obama had laid down a huge marker to his Arab audience, that he would be able to press Israel to stop building settlements in the occupied territories. It was not entirely clear how he would accomplish this. Moreover, the last two presidents waited until late in their terms before investing their dwindling political capital in pursuit of a peace settlement. They calculated, presumably, that the status quo, however uneasy, was preferable to a costly failure to achieve what many observers thought was unachievable anyway. Obama, in contrast, appeared to have calculated that the status quo is on an incline to catastrophe.

Events, meanwhile, appeared to have wrong-footed the administration's diplomatic strategy for countering Iran's nuclear ambitions. On March 20, 2009, the president had delivered videotaped New Year's greetings to the Iranian people and, conspicuously, to the clerical regime, which he addressed as the "Islamic Republic of Iran." This was seen as confirmation that he was not going to contest the legitimacy of a regime with which he hoped to negotiate a settlement of the nuclear dispute. The problem with this strategy, however, became obvious a few days after the June 4 Cairo speech. It was precisely the regime's legitimacy that millions of Iranians themselves questioned in the weeks of stirring, and brutally repressed, street demonstrations after President Mahmoud Ahmadinejad's preposterous reelection margin was announced.

In the initial days of protests and repression, the U.S. administration's response was decidedly low key. This posture was attacked by Republicans, including notably John McCain, for positioning the United States on the wrong side of history. The United States was certainly more cautious in its statements than many of its European allies, including France and the United Kingdom. But Obama clearly believed, as he stated repeatedly, that although America's ostentatious association with the protestors might make Americans feel better, it could discredit and undermine the protestors themselves, who had taken great care to adorn their rebellion with the symbols and rhetoric of Islamic piety and Iranian nationalism. As compelling as his logic might have been, however, Obama's diffidence was probably unsustainable, and as the repression became more brutal, he spoke out against it more forcefully. The administration still maintained that it was ready for engagement with the Iranian regime. Yet, aside from the moral costs of such engagement, there was real doubt whether the turmoil in Iran left its leaders in any position, or mood, to reciprocate. Netanyahu had returned to Israel from his White House meeting in May 2009 claiming that Obama had conceded an end-of-year deadline for engaging Iran, beyond which the United States would have to try something else. In reality, Obama had offered no hard deadline, but it was nonetheless true that many administration officials defended the policy of engagement as laying the groundwork, if engagement were to be shown to have failed, for organizing a stronger international coalition to impose tougher sanctions.

This volume is a book of explanation and a book of warning. Among its purposes is to explain in concise terms the complex connections between Iran's nuclear threats, the Israel—Palestine tragedy, and the Obama administration's strategies for rebuilding America's position in the Middle East. We, the authors, are broadly sympathetic to those strategies, but we are also realistic about their chances for success. We have tried to avoid the cant and vitriol that characterizes so much discussion of Middle East policy: from the neoconservatives for whom reality devolves to a war against "Islamo-fascism," to the anti-Zionists who see Israel at the root of all Middle East evil. Our book comes out in the second year of the Obama administration, under the shadow of two real wars and one impending one. Iraq simmers at a lower level of conflict, which offers hope but no assurance that most U.S. troops can be withdrawn, as promised, by December 2011 without precipitating renewed carnage. Afghanistan, meanwhile, remains unstable, and the administration's December 2009 decision to commit more troops there makes the whole problem look eerily—pitfalls of historical analogy notwithstanding—like Obama's Vietnam. It is easy to see, under these circumstances, why the administration is loath to contemplate a third front in the Islamic world that could be opened by Israeli air strikes against Iran. If that war comes, we hope our readers will be better positioned to understand why. If the war can be avoided, they should appreciate how much more work is needed to establish a stable peace.

We offer no simple solutions, either to the Iranian nuclear challenge or to the Israel—Palestine tragedy, because there are none. But there are bad options and disastrous ones, and the historical syndromes and security dilemmas of the major players are boxing us into the territory of disaster. The rumors of war are growing more insistent—and this war, we are convinced, will be different from past wars in the Middle East. It will be different because it is a thread in a tangle of crises, and when the thread is tugged, the hopes that Obama has embodied may unravel.

This short book proceeds from setting out the problems and dangers in their Iranian, Israeli, and Arab dimensions, to describing the complexities and failures, so far, of diplomatic efforts to solve these problems, to explaining Obama administration's hopes for a game-changing shift in U.S. policy toward the Middle East. It concludes with a second-year assessment of the Obama policies, and recommendations for rescuing their failures and consolidating their successes. Chapter 1, "Iran's Uranium," lays out the technical and political aspects of the nuclear threat, with due attention to the deadly misperceptions engendered by the last 30 tortuous years of U.S.—Iranian relations. Chapter 2, "Israel's Panic," explains how the Israeli reaction to this threat is clouding its strategic vision, complicating its ability to grapple with the corrosive consequences of a four-decades-long occupation of Palestinian territory, threatening to strain relations with the United

States, and moving it in the direction of a potentially destabilizing military attack. Chapter 3, "The Arabs' Cold War," describes the acute tension between Arab regimes' fear of a nuclear Iran, and Arab publics' anger at Israel's occupation and the perceived double standard by which Israel is accorded a nuclear monopoly in the region. The chapter also assesses the possible regional ramifications of military action, a wider war engulfing Arab states and the United States. Chapter 4, "Diplomacy's Struggle," sketches the history of diplomatic efforts to rein in Iran's nuclear ambitions, involving the major European powers plus Russia and China. It also draws the broader connections to global strategic hopes and fears: hopes that the world might actually start moving toward complete nuclear disarmament; fears (currently more plausible) that we are on the verge of a world of 15 or 20 nuclear states, in which a nuclear war, somewhere and sometime, would seem almost inevitable. Chapter 5, "Obama's Gamble," explains the new administration's strategy toward the Middle East, Israel, and Iran, and assesses the likelihood of success. And it lays out the stakes. Failure could bring disaster not only in the Middle East and Israel in particular, but a chain reaction that would create a failed presidency and sabotage the great hopes for a commonsense, liberal restoration in American politics and foreign policy.

Chapter 1

Iran's Uranium

"Iran is really only an honorary member of the Axis of
Evil."

—Walter Slocombe, conference remarks, January 2003, Brussels

THE THREE DECADES OF ANTAGONISM BETWEEN THE
United States and the Islamic Republic of Iran have
been mixed with a few moments of seeming missed
opportunity. One of the most recent followed 9/11. Iran's
reformist president Mohammad Khatami expressed "deep
sympathy to the American nation" for their horrific losses
in New York and Washington, while thousands of Iranians joined candlelight vigils of solidarity. The emotional
convergence was followed by real strategic cooperation.
Iran and the United States had a common enemy in the

Taliban, and Tehran assisted U.S. operations in Afghanistan by opening its airspace to American planes, agreeing to rescue downed U.S. pilots, and providing port facilities for the flow of aid to Afghan refugees. In December 2001, at the Bonn Conference to form a post-Taliban government, Iran's diplomats played an important role in persuading Northern Alliance leader Burhanuddin Rabbani to step aside for Washington's preferred candidate for president, Hamid Karzai.[1]

About a month after the Bonn Conference, President George W. Bush's "Axis of Evil" speech—a charter document of Bush's foreign policy doctrine—appeared to close the window on this rapprochement. The president warned against being fooled by the tactical quiet of hostile regimes after September 11, because "we know their true nature." He bracketed Iran between North Korea, "arming with missiles and weapons of mass destruction, while starving its citizens," and an Iraq "that has already used poison gas to murder thousands of its own citizens—leaving the bodies of mothers huddled over their dead children." Iran got one sentence. It "aggressively pursues these weapons [of mass destruction]," said Bush, "and exports terror, while an unelected few repress the Iranian people's hope for freedom." Bush continued:

> States like these, and their terrorist allies, constitute an axis of evil, arming to threaten the peace of the world. By seeking weapons of mass destruction, these regimes pose a grave and growing danger. They could provide these arms to terrorists, giving them the means to match their hatred. They could attack our allies or attempt to blackmail the United States. In any of these cases, the price of indifference would be catastrophic.[2]

The "Axis of Evil" address marked out a disastrous course for American foreign policy—abandoning the fundamental strategic principle that it is better to divide one's enemies than to combine them. Bush followed that course first into Iraq, where the only significant link between Saddam Hussein and Osama bin Laden was that they were both bad. This fallacy of strategic conflation—a characteristic Bush administration error—seemed equally perverse in the case of Iran. Recent wars of Iran and the United States had revealed overlapping interests against common enemies: the Taliban with their al-Qaeda guests, and Saddam Hussein himself.[3] This was part of the meaning of the joke, supplying the epigraph above, from Walter Slocombe (a former high-level Pentagon official in the Clinton administration who was about to be appointed as a key occupation official in Iraq). Indeed, even after President Bush's speech there was some readiness in both Washington and Tehran to cooperate in taking down Saddam's regime.[4]

In fairness to Bush, however, he knew something in January 2002 that most did not. The U.S. intelligence community was certainly aware by this time of information that was to be revealed publicly in August 2002 by an exile Iranian terrorist group, and then confirmed the following year by the UN's International Atomic Energy Agency in Vienna. Iran was secretly building a nuclear fuel enrichment facility at Natanz and a heavy water production plant at Arak. Evidence that was later made public indicated that the Iranians were also working on a nuclear warhead design.[5]

The nuclearization of Iran—a vague term, to be sure, but parsed below—constitutes a reckless and frightening escalation of the shadow conflicts and real wars in the Middle East. Whatever else we will argue in this book, and however misguided some American and Israeli choices may have been, Iran's culpability for a fundamental threat "to international peace and security" (the repeated judgment of the UN Security Council)[6] cannot be ignored and should not be obscured. Tehran has been offered several ways out of this confrontation. It has been unwilling—or perhaps unable—to follow the exit signs.

Intelligence Test

The fiasco of Iraq undoubtedly shadows the problem of Iran. *Intelligence failure* does not begin to capture the many blunders of strategy, diplomacy, military planning and postconflict preparation, domestic politics, and common sense that contributed to America's misadventure.[7] Many or most of these fundamental errors would have been mistakes even if widespread assumptions about Iraq's chemical and biological weapons stores, and nuclear weapons program, had proven to be true.

That these assumptions were utterly false, however, discredited not only the Iraq war but also tends to discredit the methods of intelligence inference that are unavoidable regarding Iran. Unsound inferences can pose traps regardless of any political or strategic agendas on the part of policy makers. One such trap concerns the problem of faulty mirror imaging: we misread an opponent's behavior because we think we know what is going on inside his head. Certainly President Bush was making a plausible inference in his September 2002 speech to the United Nations General Assembly when he said, "We know that Saddam Hussein pursued weapons of mass murder even when inspectors were in his country. Are we to assume that he stopped when they left?"[8]

The force of "history, the logic and the facts"—as Bush put it in the same speech—was strengthened by Saddam's subsequent behavior while coalition forces massed on his borders. Surely, one might infer, the best way out of the trap that was being laid would be to prove that he was not hiding the weapons that he did not, in fact, possess. Yet it is precisely here that the misleading dynamics of mirror imaging can lead astray. Not only did we make questionable assumptions about the rationality and coherence of Saddam's worldview, but there were also unproven assumptions about the rationality of *our own* behavior. Is it irrefutably the case, for example, that the United States would have called off the invasion if it were known that the "weapons of mass destruction" constituting the *casus belli* did not exist?

Since we are unable to answer that question with much confidence, we must be wary about concluding that Saddam's actions, while undoubtedly evil, were also— in his own terms—illogical. As David Hannay, a former U.K. ambassador to the UN, has observed, well before this final crisis, the Iraqi dictator had good reason to conclude that the United States was bent on removing him from power even if he fulfilled all UN demands.[9] Moreover, there were other obstacles to a clear view on the part of Iraq's leadership of its own action and consequences. During his interrogation in the five months between capture and hanging, Saddam suggested that his fear of revealing weakness to Iran was reason enough to avoid disclosing the truth about Iraq's weapons programs to the world.[10] Whether or not the captive dictator's own last words on the subject can be considered conclusive, they do suggest another intelligence failure, on Saddam's part, of fateful consequence for the Iraqi leadership's capacity to distinguish between imminent and long-term threats.

Dictatorships—dependent as they are on suppressing debate, and often murderously so—may be particularly bad at accessing a reliable picture of the reality around them. (An earlier theory, based on interviews with Iraqi weapons scientists in the first months after regime change, posited that Saddam himself might have been unaware—because it was too dangerous to tell him—that the weapons programs had not been reconstituted.)[11]

What is disturbing now is that all of these elements of pride and bluff, self-delusion and truth-obscuring tyranny can be seen to operate in Iran as well.[12] It is not possible to make sensible policy about Iran's nuclear program without inferring something about its purpose. But we do, at the same time, have to recognize the limits of our intelligence. This recognition helps explain the caution of the U.S. intelligence community on the subject. In late 2007, the National Intelligence Council released the declassified version of key findings in their latest "National Intelligence Estimate" (NIE) regarding Iran's nuclear program. The most surprising, and controversial, finding stated the following:

> We judge with high confidence that in fall 2003, Tehran halted its nuclear weapons program; we also assess with moderate-to-high confidence that Tehran at a minimum is keeping open the option to develop nuclear weapons. We judge with high confidence that the halt, and Tehran's announcement of its decision to suspend its declared uranium enrichment program and sign an Additional Protocol to its Nuclear Non-Proliferation Treaty Safeguards Agreement, was directed primarily in response to increasing international scrutiny and pressure resulting from exposure of Iran's previously undeclared nuclear work.[13]

The NIE was much misunderstood and widely misrepresented. Its definition of "nuclear weapons program" was a narrow one, and the second clause about Iran "keeping open the options" was of equal or greater importance. Contrary to much speculation, the findings were not released as an intelligence community broadside against the Bush administration in retaliation for alleged politicization of the Iraq intelligence estimates—the decision to release this one was, in fact, President Bush's.[14] Republican critics, such as Henry Kissinger, complained that the intelligence community with this estimate had "venture[d] into policy conjecture," thereby turning itself into "a kind of check on, instead of a part of, the executive branch."[15] Yet the main conclusion about Iran's weaponization halt, that it was "a response to increasing international scrutiny and pressure," clearly pertained to a legitimate and important intelligence question—how could they be stopped?[16]

"Everyone thinks their goal is a nuclear weapon," a senior U.S. intelligence analyst told us, referring to his colleagues in the intelligence community. "But Iran is playing a long game."[17] Ambiguity, and Iran's ability to play a long game, is tied to the nature of nuclear technology. Tehran, in defiance of UN Security Council resolutions, has been working to master the nuclear *fuel cycle* by learning to spin thousands of industrial centrifuges at the supersonic speeds required to enrich uranium. This enriched uranium is the fissile material that constitutes the most difficult-to-obtain element of a nuclear weapon (the other elements are a workable warhead design, on which, according to the U.S. intelligence community, Iran stopped work, at least for a while, and the delivery vehicles, such as the missiles that Iran very definitely is continuing to develop and test).[18]

Enriched uranium can also be used as fuel for nuclear reactors, which is what the Iranians claim they are working toward. They claim that the Islamic Republic's successive supreme leaders—the ayatollahs Khomeini and Khamenei—have ruled that nuclear weapons violate the precepts of Islam. Fareed Zakaria, of *Newsweek International,* argues that claims based on these alleged rulings cannot be dismissed as irrelevant because it would be politically difficult within the regime to act in open defiance of them.[19] (To be sure, taking them seriously also conjures up yet another intelligence failure of black-comic dimensions: in an interview seven months before the Iraq war, Iraqi Foreign Minister Tariq Aziz expressed amazement that Britain would really join an invasion—given that the Archbishop of Canterbury had come out against military action.)[20]

There is room, in any event, for argument about what Iran is up to. Its leaders might be prepared to stop the nuclear program someplace short of actually building and deploying nuclear weapons. But there are three problems. First, Iran has been caught cheating on its obligations under the NPT; among the secrets that were uncovered was evidence of work on a nuclear weapon design.[21] In February 2010 the normally cautious International Atomic Energy Agency (IAEA) issued a report noting concerns about Iranian development of a nuclear warhead.[22] Second, the supposedly peaceful purpose of the nuclear program is belied by its economic illogic: the vast effort and expense of industrial-scale enrichment would pay off only if Iran was building multiple nuclear power stations, but there is no sign of them. There are simpler and safer international sources of supply for nuclear fuel. Finally, and most fundamentally, Iran can eat its nuclear cake and have it too. By mastering the fuel cycle and enriching uranium on a large scale, Iran turns itself into a "virtual" nuclear weapons state. It would be only a short step—and a matter of months or even weeks—between this virtual status and crossing the line to building weapons.

Ambiguous intelligence contributed to a war in Iraq, and something similar could happen in Iran. That said, it is necessary to remember a critical difference: the most important and most difficult component of a nuclear weapons capability—Iran's uranium enrichment program—is the one element of Iran's activities that is indisputable and undisputed. While uncertainty should be taken seriously, it cannot be grounds for complacency, because there is hardly any doubt that Iran's defiant march toward a nuclear capability is creating the objective conditions for a descent into war. Even if the Iranian leadership has not made the final decision to weaponize, by building the capabilities for a condition of "nuclear latency," coming so close to a weapons capability while engaging in rhetoric about the illegitimacy and impermanence of the "Zionist regime," Iran is creating a mood of panic in Israel that creates, in Sam Gardiner's memorable phrase, an "excess demand" for military action.[23]

Indeed, Israeli officials and the Bush administration both used to argue that developed enrichment technology constituted the "point of no return" beyond which Iran would have to be considered a nuclear threat. They stopped talking this way after the red line was crossed. Iran already has enough low-enriched uranium for at least one nuclear weapon, if further enriched.

The intelligence problem of whether Iran intends to build actual nuclear weapons is tied up with the broader questions of why it might want them and what it would do if it acquired them. In trying to answer these questions, we should avoid the trap of assuming that states, any more than individuals, are driven by simple or unitary motivations. (It is fair to assume, moreover, that fractured regimes, like conflicted individuals, are especially prone to complex and multiple motives.) In the heated debate about Iran's nuclear drive, four purposes are most commonly suggested: to destroy Israel and annihilate Israelis; to protect the Iranian regime and nation against foreign aggression and hegemony; to serve as intimidating instruments of *Iranian* aggression and hegemony; and to bolster Iranians' techno-nationalist pride. The first purpose seems highly implausible but cannot be removed from the discussion, for reasons considered below. The fourth does not require weaponization but does not preclude it either. As for the second and third, there is no reason that defensive and offensive purposes cannot go hand in hand.

This is an obvious point, but it derives special resonance from the traumatic and foundational war that marked the Islamic Republic's first decade. On September 22, 1980, Saddam Hussein's Iraqi forces invaded Iran. Saddam hoped, in the turmoil following the fall of the Shah, to exploit the demoralization of Iran's regular army and perhaps even to ignite a popular revolt that would topple the new regime. He was emboldened by early successes: the fall of Khorramshahr and the sieges of Abadan and Ahvaz. Within two months, however, Iran had mounted counteroffensives of astonishing ferocity: human-wave assaults conducted by Revolutionary Guard and Basij units with the seemingly endless fodder of Iranian youths. Thousands were killed or maimed, but the assaults were effective, opening ground for regular army forces to move forward.

Iraq reacted by using chemical weapons for mass killing, a macabre violation of the laws of war that was greeted with general indifference from the world community. Iran's leaders were properly horrified as Iraq unleashed chemical weapons not only against Iranian troops, but also against Iraqi Kurds in Halabja. Those of us who monitored the Iran-Iraq War for the U.S. government will not easily forget Iraq's chilling communiqué, around the time of the Second Battle of al-Faw, which stated that "for every insect there is the proper insecticide."

But the United States, as a practical matter, condoned the use of these weapons against Iranians. Its formal condemnations were tepid and ostentatiously even-handed. An April 1984 National Security Decision Directive approved by President Reagan emphasized, "Our condemnation of the use of CW munitions by the belligerents should place equal stress on the urgent need to dissuade Iran from continuing the ruthless and inhumane tactics which have characterized recent offensives."[24] Presidential envoy Donald Rumsfeld traveled to Baghdad for a second time in 1984 with written instructions that he should reiterate to Iraq's foreign minister Aziz earlier assurances from Secretary of State George Schultz that a U.S. statement condemning the use of chemical weapons "was made strictly out of our strong opposition to the use of lethal and incapacitating CW, wherever it occurs." But the United States's "interests in 1) preventing an Iranian victory and 2) continuing to improve bilateral relations with Iraq, at a pace of Iraq's choosing, remain undiminished."[25] Moreover, it is probably a good thing that Tehran did not have any insight into the interagency process regarding the question of sanctions against Iraq for its use of chemical weapons against its own civilians at Halabja. The Reagan administration gave Iraq what could best be described as a suspended sentence.

Iraq's use of chemical weapons was strategically significant.[26] With the advent of the so-called war of the cities, in which Iraq launched missile attacks against Iranian population centers, the revolutionary leadership foresaw the inevitable combination of ballistic missiles and chemical weapons and concluded that the bitter cup of defeat had to be imbibed.[27]

Although the origins of Iran's nuclear program lie in Pahlavi rule, the impetus supplied by the Iran-Iraq War is evident. Iranians certainly remember that the rest of the world effectively shrugged when Iraq used a so-called weapon of mass destruction against them, and they also remember America's de facto alliance with Saddam. U.S. companies sold Iraq precursors useable for chemical weapons, while Washington helped Baghdad locate third-country sources for purchase of weapons, such as cluster bombs, that the United States was unable to provide; provided satellite intelligence on the positioning of Iran's forces; and reflagged and protected Kuwaiti oil tankers after the Islamic Revolutionary Guard Corps started to attack the Gulf Arab shipping that was helping to finance Iraq's war effort.[28] This brought the United States Navy into frequent skirmishes with Iranian small gunboats. And on a hot, tense day in July 1988, having just sunk two vessels that were shooting at American helicopters, the USS *Vincennes* fired two missiles at Iran Air Flight 655, which had just taken off from Bandar Abbas en route to Dubai. All 290 passengers, including 66 children, were killed. The destruction of the commercial airliner was an accident; clearly the Vincennes' captain believed that his radar was showing an attacking military aircraft. Just as clearly, many Iranians continue to believe that the American destruction of a packed civilian airplane was deliberate. Iran expert Ray Takeyh has argued that the downing of Iran Air Flight 655 "appears to have been the catalyst that convinced Khomeini that it was time to end the war." The imam and those around him perceived that America, siding with Iraq, had now "decided to finish the job itself."[29] As events transpired more than a decade later, of course, it was Iran's enemies—the Taliban regime in Kabul and Ba'athist regime in Baghdad—whom the Americans destroyed. These were huge strategic gifts to Iran, but with the unwelcome side effect that the Iranians were now encircled by the armed forces of a superpower that had included them on a list of the world's intolerable regimes. Against this background, Iran's determination to obtain nuclear weapons capability is not surprising.

Understanding this motivation does not mean condoning it. Iran was in many ways a victim—of Iraqi atrocities and American hostility—but it was hardly an *innocent* victim. The eight-year war that started with an Iraqi invasion was in some significant measure generated by Khomeini's internationalist revolutionary fervor. The Arab monarchies and dictatorships to Tehran's south and west were undisguised targets of that fervor. Since at least the Napoleonic convulsions of Europe, the link between internal revolution and external war has been evident.[30] However distasteful it was to back Saddam, the Reagan administration was not wrong to view Iraq's Ba'athist regime as a critical barrier to the internationalization of the Islamic revolution. Moreover, the human-wave tactics employed by Iran *were* "ruthless and inhumane," as the Reagan directive had argued, though the administration was wrong to equate them with the use of chemical weapons.

So this history explains not just an understandable Iranian motivation for acquiring nuclear weapons capability; it also reminds us of why the rest of the world cannot contemplate the prospect with equanimity. A common academic view holds that Iran has demonstrated a prudent and conservative foreign policy whenever the basic interests or survival of the regime might be at stake. There is evidence for this generalization—most strikingly, perhaps, in the Ayatollah Khomeini's difficult decision to end the Iran-Iraq war on terms that he found humiliating. But the regime's conduct of foreign affairs has hardly been an unalloyed model of prudence, as the prelude to and conduct of the war with Iraq indicates. Khomeini's revolutionary fanaticism was genuine, and genuinely frightening. It has set posthumous limits on efforts by some of Iran's leaders to satisfy the clear yearnings of many Iranians to live in a more normal country.

The Reagan administration's decision, in the face of such fanaticism, to align with Iraq certainly exposed the United States to charges of hypocrisy when, two decades later, George W. Bush was waxing indignant about the "bodies of mothers huddled over their dead children" after Iraqi chemical weapons attacks. For Washington such inconsistency, if not hypocrisy, may be inevitable in balancing competing interests. But for understanding Iran's motives and psychology, we should at least appreciate that our own double standards—and inability to grasp how these look to their victims—can contribute to yet another intelligence failure.

Satan and Zion

In 1979 radical Islam intruded into Washington's Cold War world. The American worldview, however, was slow to adapt to what Lawrence Freedman calls the "second radical wave," which succeeded and gradually supplanted the Arab world's militant secular nationalism—but impelled this time by non-Arab Iran.[31] The seemingly tight fit of the prior generation's secular radicalism into the Cold War template was no doubt a key reason why it was so hard for Washington to grasp the implications of the radical wave launched by the Iranian revolution. The complex mixture of factors that impeded Washington's ability to act effectively and constructively in the Middle East after 1979 was to be compounded during the George W. Bush administration by the disorienting shock of the September 11 attacks and the ideological rigidity and incompetence of key officials. In consequence, the United States eventually found itself at odds with everyone: Iran, Iraqi factions, and al-Qaeda—true strategic failure.

Freedman in 2008 published a magisterial anatomy of that failure, *A Choice of Enemies*, which takes the Iranian revolution as its starting point. Other junctures, such as the Suez Crisis of 1956, the year of revolutions in 1958, the Six-Day War of 1967, or even the Yom Kippur War of 1973, might recommend themselves as alternatives. Yet it wasn't really until the 1980s that U.S. strategic and military involvement in the region began to deepen, and as a consequence of two geographically proximate but crucially distinct events—the fall of the Shah and, 11 months later, the Soviet invasion of Afghanistan. President Jimmy Carter's response to these events, more fateful than it may have appeared at the time, was to declare that "an attempt by any outside force to gain control of the Persian Gulf region will be regarded as an assault on the vital interests of the United States of America, and such an assault will be repelled by any means necessary, including military force."[32] This Carter Doctrine laid the conceptual basis for an American commitment that continues today with wars in Iraq and Afghanistan. At the time, no Washington policy maker could have conceived of, say, a U.S. army of 150,000 troops situated in any Middle Eastern country, let alone Iraq. Gradually the idea acquired plausibility. The creation of the Rapid Deployment Joint Task Force—now the Central Command recently headed by General David Petraeus—provided the means to implement the Carter Doctrine.

This was also the time when America's *emotional* involvement in the region began to deepen, in ways that were not entirely healthy. In particular, the grudge match with Iran was to frame American views of the Middle East for the next 3 decades. America's political and moral commitment to Israel was longstanding, of course, but for U.S. policy makers concerned about regional rivalry with the Soviets, the circumstances of a Jewish state in a sea of Arabs did not constitute an unalloyed strategic asset; hence there was interest in nurturing at least an illusion of detachment. Events following the Iranian revolution shattered that illusion. Most traumatic, of course, was the seizure and humiliating 444 days of captivity for 52 American hostages in the U.S. embassy in Tehran. Freedman argues that President Carter made a mistake by elevating the crisis "to the highest level from day one," with the result that "his ineffectuality became a more salient factor than his human decency."[33] It is debatable, however, that in the climate of wounded American nationalism it would have been possible to downplay the crisis. What is clear is that the president's political demise, which had multiple causes in any event, also carried with it a significant impact on the American national psychology, an insidious injection of resentment verging on rage toward a region that Americans poorly understood, but in which they were increasingly entangled.

The entanglement exposed America to, among other problems, the fires of terrorism, initially fueled and directed by an Iranian revolutionary regime that would consistently use terror as its paramount instrument of conflict with Israel and the West (though it is worth remembering that at the same time the United States was backing Iraq in its war against Iran).[34] The first suicide bombing to grab Americans' attention—at least since the Japanese kamikazes of the Second World War—came in the form of an explosives-laden truck that burst into the Marines Corps compound in Beirut at 6:22 in the morning of October 23, 1983. The explosion killed the driver, 1 Lebanese civilian, and 241 marines and other U.S. personnel. Two minutes later, a second truck bomb killed 58 French paratroopers in their own compound across the city. Both contingents—which had been deployed to Lebanon to keep peace after Israel's invasion and the PLO's evacuation, but increasingly were seen as backing Maronite Christians in their civil war against Lebanon's Shi'a—were withdrawn within four months. French President François Mitterrand ordered a retaliatory air strike against Islamic Revolutionary Guard Corps positions in the Bekaa Valley. The Reagan administration, together with Paris, considered attacks against Lebanese barracks housing Iran's Islamic Revolutionary Guards and a camp where the truck bombings were believed to have been planned. After some desultory naval bombardment and air attacks, however, Reagan decided against any significant retaliation; together with the Marines' withdrawal, this decision has been branded, by those who tend toward a censorious attitude about American resolve, as the original sin in U.S. appeasement of Islamic terrorism.[35] More directly damaging to Reagan's reputation, however, was the actual payment three years later of ransom for Lebanese-held hostages, in the form of arms sales to an Iranian regime that was desperate for weapons to use against Iraq. The Americans' own desperation to free the hostages was all-too-understandable, given that one of them—former

Beirut CIA station chief William Buckley—was being tortured to death. But Buckley died, the few hostages successfully ransomed were soon replaced by others, and when the affair blew up Tehran was able to gloat about how it had suckered Washington.[36] (The extra zeal of the gloating was pretty obviously a defense against intraregime recriminations about dealings with Americans.) The Iran-*contra* affair had its bizarre dimension—Col. Oliver North's side operation of diverting profits from the arms sales to anti-Sandinista rebels in Nicaragua—and its ever-to-be-remembered surreal detail—the chocolate cake that North and Robert "Bud" McFarlane, Reagan's national security adviser, carried, along with a bible signed by Reagan, to be presented as gifts upon deplaning in Tehran. The comic ineptitude of the whole thing made the strategic thinking behind it seem like a flimsy pretext, which perhaps it was. Still, whatever the main motives, and however ill-conceived the actual operation, the idea of probing for engagement with more moderate Iranian factions, and perhaps even mediating a settlement of the war with Iraq, was not crazy. After the scandal broke, however—with ensuing congressional hearings, criminal convictions, and McFarlane's attempted suicide—the idea was largely discredited.

The most consequential phase of deepening America's strategic commitment to the Middle East was set in motion, after the end of the Iran-Iraq war, by Saddam Hussein's peculiar notion that the world in general and America in particular would simply swallow his invasion of Kuwait. Disabusing him of this notion involved a process in which everything seemed to go right for American power. With astonishing diplomatic skill, the George H. W. Bush administration assembled a truly global coalition against the invaders. It spanned a spectrum, in the Middle East, from Syria to (albeit tacitly) Israel. It included, globally, a Soviet leadership that was remarkably forgiving about its recent humiliation by U.S.-backed *mujahideen* in nearby Afghanistan. The step-change in U.S. military technology and force-projection capabilities, and the seeming ease with which these were employed to eject Iraq from Kuwait, awed even the Americans themselves (it helped that Saddam committed his blunder before the bulk of U.S. forces had been withdrawn from convenient staging bases in Germany). We know now that some dangerous processes of recoil were being set up. Russia became focused on a narrative of Western betrayal of the Cold War settlement. In Iraq, although the UN's postwar sanctions regime was successful in its own terms—together with inspections and occasional air strikes, it prevented reconstitution of WMD—it was devastating to the Iraqi people. In Saudi Arabia, the deployment of U.S. forces bred fundamentalist anger. In Afghanistan, empowerment of fundamentalist factions contributed to civil war following Soviet withdrawal and American disengagement. At the time, however, it was easy to imagine that American military power had provided overwhelmingly positive impulse for happier developments in the Middle East and beyond. The Bush administration was able to convene a Madrid conference at which a large number of Arab states for the first time sat at a table with Israel. Secret meetings between Israelis and Palestinians had started in Oslo without American involvement; arguably, however, America's defeat of Saddam, whom Yasir Arafat and other Palestinians had loudly cheered, introduced more healthy realism to Palestinian calculations.

With both the Bush and Clinton administrations' overriding focus now on promoting peace between Arabs and Israelis, there was limited American interest in any theoretical possibilities of detente with Iran. Saddam was "in the box" (the then-current Washington expression), while Syria was ready for talks with Israel. So Iran stood out, and stands out today, as the lodestar of bloody-minded rejection. President Ali Rafsanjani was ready in the late 1980s and early 1990s to talk about Iran's desire to reintegrate with the global economy, to help organize the release of the last American hostages in Lebanon, and to declare that detente with Washington "would not be in contradiction with Iran's objectives."[37] But Rafsanjani also joined in blood-curdling rhetoric against Israel's existence, while Iran officially lauded and covertly aided the suicide bombing of Israeli civilians. After Oslo, Iran added to its rhetorical targets the Palestinian leaders, who were excoriated as dupes and traitors. And Tehran's gloating over Israeli Prime Minister Yitzhak Rabin's assassination at the hands of a right-wing Israeli could not have been better calculated to get under the skin of an openly emotional President Bill Clinton.

These were the circumstances in which the Clinton administration embraced two conceptually shaky ideas: a category of "rogue states" in which Iran was included (questionable because it implied just a few aberrant hold-outs from a general movement of progressive globalization), and the declared strategy of "dual containment" against Iraq and Iran (shaky because it was simply a tall order to abandon the previous strategy of balancing one against the other). Containment of Iran had an economic dimension in America's cutoff of commercial ties between the two countries, which had grown to a surprising degree after President Reagan lifted the trading ban in 1982.[38] An enthusiastic U.S. Congress—in Republican hands from January 1995—included in its Iran-Libya Sanctions Act penalties against foreign companies investing in Iran's energy sector that also had business in the United States. Had President Clinton not invoked the usual get-out clause that such extraterritorial sanctions legislation almost always contains (in declining to enforce those provisions, he was able to cite overriding "national interest"), the sanctions might have posed a significant threat to Iran's economy, not to mention the effect on transatlantic comity. In the event, Iran was able to compensate with trade and significant investment from Europe. Tehran was nonetheless rattled by Washington's efforts at economic containment, and not inclined to see the American military presence—in Saudi Arabia, in the Persian Gulf, in Turkey and in the air over Iraq—as dictating Iranian caution. On the contrary, the Islamic Revolutionary Guards Corps engaged in some truly shocking risk taking, using their favorite tool of terrorism to warn America to back off. After casing targets in multiple places, they used a truck bomb in 1996 to attack Khobar Towers, a complex near the Saudi coast that housed U.S. military personnel. This massive explosion killed 19 people. The attack was convincingly tied to Iranian operatives.

In the aftermath of Khobar, Iran and the United States came close to war. Clinton officials were somewhat taken aback when Chairman of the Joint Chiefs General John Shalikashvili briefed them on CENTCOM contingency plans for a land invasion by Army and Marine divisions and a bombing campaign against port facilities and air force and missile installations. The White House aides asked for more limited options that would nonetheless destroy high-value targets. The idea, recalled Richard Clarke, Clinton's counterterrorism czar (with whom one of this book's coauthors worked at the time) was to borrow from "the old nuclear strategy concept of escalation dominance...where you hit the guy the first time so hard, where he loses something he really values, and then you tell him if he responds, he will lose everything else he values." Instead of a direct military option, however, the United States conducted an operation involving numerous CIA assets and "a more or less simultaneous series of intelligence actions around the world." According to Clarke, "Following the intelligence operation, and perhaps because of it and the serious U.S. threats, among other reasons, Iran ceased terrorism against the U.S. War with Iran was averted."[39]

It is likely, however, that "other reasons" Clarke alludes to were most important. The intelligence operation directed against Iran would probably not have affected the Revolutionary Guard officers who stage-managed the Khobar attack. War was averted because Saudi Arabia, which had also been targeted, would not stand for it, and because decisive evidence failed to emerge before internal changes in Iran took retaliation off the table. The concurrent rise of the Islamic Republic's first meaningful reform movement, which was able, in the election of 1997, to elevate the liberal cleric Mohammad Khatami to Iran's presidency, helped to calm the covert conflict with America. Khatami's election opened the most significant window of opportunity for improving U.S.-Iranian relations since 1979, and the Clinton administration, despite congressional restraints and its own vulnerabilities on the hawkish right, did make some effort to squeeze through it. Secretary of State Madeleine Albright offered a guarded apology for America's neocolonial transgressions including, most significantly, the CIA-orchestrated coup that had toppled Prime Minister Mohammad Mossadeq in 1953. Khatami, for his part, issued his plea for a "dialogue of civilizations." These concededly limited attempts to establish a *modus vivendi* facilitated the rather close cooperation in Afghanistan in the wake of September 11. But they were derailed by, among other things, Washington's conviction that Iran was sheltering al-Qaeda fugitives who were still supervising or, at a minimum, cheerleading, attacks against American allies.[40] Catching Tehran covertly shipping a huge quantity of weapons and explosives to Yasir Arafat during the *intifada* reinforced U.S. perceptions that Iran remained wedded to a radical agenda. Rapprochement at that point was probably not in the cards, but Bush's designation of Iran as a member of the 'axis of evil' no doubt precluded the possibility. And then there were the revelations about nuclear enrichment.[41]

There was, however, a final, tantalizing bid from the Khatami government for talks to normalize U.S.-Iranian relations. It came in the form of a May 2003 memo that was passed on to Washington by the Swiss Ambassador in Tehran, Tim Guldimann, who represented U.S. interests in Iran. It proposed talks aimed at a kind of grand bargain, whereby Iran might restrain its nuclear ambitions, end its support for terrorism, coordinate policies in Iraq, and endorse a two-state solution to the Israel-Palestine conflict in exchange for American undertakings to lift sanctions and recognize Iran's regional security interests. There is no doubt about the authenticity of the document, or that it was authorized by Khatami possibly with the approval of Supreme Leader Khamenei. More debatable is whether the Khatami government was in any position to carry through on the proposal. There was no excuse, however, for the Bush administration's failure to pursue it. U.S. Secretary of State Colin Powell and his deputy, Richard Armitage, urged President Bush to reply favorably; Vice President Dick Cheney and Secretary of Defense Donald Rumsfeld argued for ignoring the demarche, and won the argument. The administration was in a triumphal mood. This was just days after President Bush had alighted, in full flight suit, from an S-3B Viking Jet that had just landed on the aircraft carrier USS *Abraham Lincoln*, to step in front of a banner emblazoned with the words "Mission Accomplished." It was probably true, of course, that any Iranian readiness for talks was inspired by the presence of victorious American troops on Iran's borders. Yet this should have been precisely the time to leverage America's good fortune, rather than assume that it would last forever.[42]

The clerical regime's bilious rhetoric and murderous policy toward Israel have been a near constant, yet successive Israeli governments, both of Likud and Labour, took a more nuanced attitude toward Iran. In the early years after the revolution, Jerusalem was trying to persuade Reagan officials that they should not overreact to Iran's bellicosity, and there was considerable unease about Washington's support for Iraq. Maintaining contacts with Tehran at various levels, Israel played a key role in drawing the administration into Iran-*contra*. Indeed, it is striking how slow Israel was to recognize the sea change brought about by the overthrow of the shah. The persistence of *periphery theory*, the idea that Israel could counterbalance its Arab neighbors by forging security ties to regimes and other actors surrounding them (Iran, but also Turkey, Ethiopia, Maronite Lebanon, and animist Sudan), blinded Israelis to the loss of Iran as a de facto ally. The fact that Israel could sustain an arms-transfer relationship with Iran, dubbed *Operation Seashell*, for several years after the revolution suggested that the dynamic of denial was reinforced by the lure of profits. (Interestingly, one of the machine guns sold by Israel to Iran was used decades later by Hezbollah in the attack that triggered the Summer War of 2006.)[43]

This somewhat murky history has been cited to argue that Israel's current alarm about Iran and its nuclear program should not "be taken at face value."[44] But, to repeat a point made earlier, nations and states rarely act on the basis of simple or unitary motivations. A nation's alarm can be very real and at the same time politically manipulated: this, we would argue, is a good summation of the psychology that led America into Iraq. Israeli officials can modulate their rhetoric regarding the existential threat posed by Iran, and there are some indications that the Netanyahu government at certain points has done so because it does not want to encourage Israeli emigration.[45] Nonetheless, numerous interviews in Israel leave little room for doubt that the fear of Iran's nuclear potential is genuine. Moreover, circumstances have changed greatly since the 1980s: Iran is moving closer to a nuclear capability; after 9/11 in the United States and waves of suicide bombings in Israel, the ideology of fear regarding a radical Islamist threat has been increasingly internalized in both American and Israeli discourse; and Khatami's reformist and relatively cosmopolitan presidency has been succeeded by the crude posturing and incendiary rhetoric of Mahmoud Ahmadinejad.

A sometimes-noted paradox of Iran is that this fountainhead of anti-Zionist invective contains the Middle East's largest remaining Jewish community outside of Israel. Though taking care not to challenge regime orthodoxy regarding Israel, the community of some 25,000 Jews abides, by most accounts, relatively unmolested, able to worship with the maximum freedom that one could expect in an Islamic theocracy.[46] It would be a mistake, however, to draw any firm policy conclusions from this situation. One might be tempted to discount the leadership's rhetoric as opportunistic and, therefore, something that can be discarded with ease. But this would be too complacent. Leading scholars of Iran are consistent in their findings that profound hatred of Israel and visceral anti-Semitism have been central to the theology, revolutionary theory, and strategic worldview of Iran's top clerical leadership. This was true of the first supreme leader, Khomeini, and remains true of the second, Khamenei. There is evidence of it, disconcertingly, in the pronouncements of the former president Rafsanjani, who more recently took personal risks as a supporter—albeit an ambiguous one—of the Green Movement. And it is certainly the case for the current president, Ahmadinejad, who replaced the conciliatory language of his predecessor, Khatami, with crude Holocaust denial and a new iteration of the Khomeini line that Israel should and will be wiped off the map.[47]

Iranians who are not necessarily Ahmadinejad enthusiasts claim that he was misinterpreted. A more accurate translation of his remarks, they say, is that Israel will "disappear from the pages of history." This can happen, as it did to the Soviet Union, without an act of war.[48] And it is true that Ahmadinejad offered similar clarifications.[49] The problem, however, is that in its 30-year history, the Islamic Republic of Iran was rarely content to be a passive witness to historical process. When the war with Iraq ended in stalemate, Khomeini determined to revive revolutionary élan with the brutal execution of thousands of political dissidents, many of whom had served their prison sentences and been released. At about the same time he issued his astonishing fatwa sanctioning the assassination of British writer Salman Rushdie—for the crime of writing a book of insufficient piety. Assassination of Iranian exiles was already by this time an established instrument of state policy. The IRGC Kuds Force deployed terrorism against victims who were simply Jewish, as opposed to "Zionist."[50] Iran continues, on a routine basis, to execute homosexuals, a cruelty in the spirit, if not the scale, of genocide.[51]

Against this background, it would be negligent to dismiss Israeli worries about a nuclear-armed Iran. Israelis know that Iran's rejectionist stance against Israel is not just a matter of words: its support for Hamas and Hezbollah has helped to kill hundreds of Israelis. Although it might seem an act of suicidal recklessness to provide the terrorists with *nuclear* weapons, no one can exclude the scenario of rogue elements among Iran's fractured decision-making apparatus behaving in a reckless manner. (There is ominous precedent for this in a neighboring country that is actually a semi-ally of the United States: the scientist AQ Khan, 'father' of Pakistan's uranium enrichment program, set up a veritable international supermarket that supplied nuclear weapons technology to rogue regimes in North Korea, Libya, and Iran itself.) Israel fears that even a virtual nuclear weapons status could embolden Iran to be more reckless and belligerent.

Taking Israel's alarm seriously does not mean, however, that we can allow ourselves to abandon all strategic perspective. Such abandonment was, to a very large extent, the American story in the first decade of the twenty-first century. The concept of an all-fronts war against Islamist extremism—and its conflation with the separate problem of Ba'athist despotism—was part of the intellectual trap that carried us into Iraq. That adventure did not go well, yet in the depths of Iraq's ensuing civil war the Bush administration and American right in general were applying the same illogic to Iran. Israel's Lebanon war in summer 2006 against Hezbollah provided an occasion for especially grandiose pronouncements in the United States. President Bush was already reformulating the "war on terrorism" as a war against "Islamo-fascism." Secretary of State Condoleezza Rice, looking on the bright side, identified the "birth pangs of a new Middle East." Former house speaker Newt Gingrich called the Lebanon war one campaign in a "third world war."

Invocations of fascism and world war are an easy breath away from charges of "appeasement"—always resonant where the Jewish state is involved—against those who allegedly fail to appreciate the magnitude of the stakes. President Bush used the occasion of Israel's 60th anniversary to level the charge against presidential candidate Barack Obama. In May 2008, in a speech before the Knesset, Bush attacked those who "seem to believe that we should negotiate with the terrorists and radicals, as if some ingenious argument will persuade them they have been wrong all along." Bush continued, "We have heard this foolish delusion before. As Nazi tanks crossed into Poland in 1939, an American senator declared: 'Lord, if I could only have talked to Hitler, all this might have been avoided.' We have an obligation to call this what it is—the false comfort of appeasement, which has been repeatedly discredited by history."[52]

The specific target of Bush's broadside was Obama's campaign promise to engage the leadership of Iran and other hostile states, if the opportunity presented itself. By this time actual Bush administration policy toward Iran was more nuanced than such rhetoric implied—it was supporting, albeit grudgingly, European efforts to negotiate with Tehran on the nuclear issue. But the Bush speech was nonetheless a ridiculous and therefore useful reminder of the limits of Churchillian resolve as the single answer to the Middle East's complex problems. There is no doubt that Iran's thuggish regime poses a serious obstacle to Middle East peacemaking and, if it develops nuclear weapons, a potentially existential threat to Israel. The tools to contain that threat must include the deterrent power of U.S. military force. But dismissing diplomacy with Iran or Syria as "appeasement" was not serious. And the idea that Israel's battles in Lebanon were to be encouraged as part of a proxy war between Washington and Tehran showed ignorance—or indifference—to the narrative impact of the televised bombing of Muslim civilians. Israel is a close ally of the United States, and the commitment to its security is a pillar of U.S. foreign policy. This does not mean, however, that Israel's security strategy and American interests always coincide. Israel has to fight its own battles, but the way it fights them can worsen America's own problems with the Arab and Islamic world. Neoconservatives saw Israel's Lebanon war as the moral and strategic equivalent of the antifascist struggle in the Spanish civil war, but many Arabs surely looked at the bombing of Dahiya as their own Guernica.

A restoration of American strategic perspective would entail better understanding of where U.S. interests and Israeli interests might diverge, and making every reasonable effort to bridge them. In the first days of the Lebanon war, that would have required—rather than egging the Israelis on—mobilizing support for the formation of an international force, deployment of the Lebanese army to the border, and presenting a workable plan to strip Hezbollah of its heavy weapons. Some of this was eventually accomplished. Israel's degradation of Hezbollah capabilities did help in this regard; the destruction of Lebanese lives and infrastructure hurt. Most damaging was Bush's insistence on portraying the fight in terms that tended to push millions of Muslims to choose the other side.

The world does have a problem with Islamist revivalism. Much of this revival is driven by local conditions, shaped by a simple but compelling set of beliefs spread by global communications, and has taken the form of a global social movement. There is no question that violent jihadism is fueled by this sort of hard Islam and that its Shi'a variant is backed by Tehran to revive its own revolution, boost Iranian influence, and challenge U.S. dominance. But the Islamist resurgence is not monolithic, and it is not something that we can be "at war" with in the sense that we can defeat it with military force.

Chapter 2

Israel's Panic

VISITORS TO ISRAELI AIR FORCE HEADQUARTERS IN TEL Aviv report frequent sightings of a striking poster. Emblazoned with the words "IAF Eagles over Auschwitz," it depicts three Israeli F-15 aircraft above the iconic gate of Birkenau, the huge death camp adjacent to Auschwitz. The poster celebrates the 2003 flyover of a Polish-Israeli commemoration of Holocaust victims 60 years earlier. The appearance of the aircraft, which left observers divided on the question of whether a show of military prowess was appropriate to the contemplative nature of the memorial service, had been more or less impromptu: the three planes were in Poland for an unrelated air show. The inspiration for joining the air force presence to the concentration camp ceremony belonged to then-brigadier general and future air force chief of staff Amir Eshel, who piloted one of the F-15s. He and his two wingmen each carried with them in their cockpits the names of all the Jews known to have perished at the Auschwitz-Birkenau complex on that day in 1943. As they barreled low through overcast skies, Eshel, whose grandmother was killed by Nazis, intoned a solemn pledge: "We pilots of the Israeli air force flying in the skies above the camp of horrors, arose from the ashes of the millions of victims and shoulder their silent cries, salute their courage, and promise to be the shield of the Jewish people and the nation Israel."[1]

The oath to be a shield to the Jewish people against another genocidal assault should be taken seriously, because planning appears to be underway to attack Iran's nuclear infrastructure should diplomacy fail to slow Tehran's quest for a weapons capability.

Will Israel Do It?

Successive Israeli governments have held that a nuclear weapons capability in the region, other than Israel's own, would pose an intolerable threat to Israel's survival as a state and society. In the early years of this decade, the Israeli government could decide, much as it did in 1981 with respect to Iraq and 2007 against Syria, to attack Iran's nuclear installations.

If Israel were to attack, it would likely concentrate on three locations: Isfahan, where Iran produces uranium hexafluoride gas; Natanz, where the gas is enriched in approximately half of the 8,000 centrifuges located there; and Arak, where a heavy water research reactor, scheduled to come on line in 2012, would be ideal to produce weapons-grade plutonium. Israel might attack other sites that it suspects to be part of a nuclear weapons program if targeting data were available, such as the recently disclosed Qom site, whose location is known, or centrifuge fabrication sites, the locations of which have not yet been publicly identified. The latter would be compelling targets because their destruction would hobble Iran's ability to reconstitute its program. But attacks against the sites at Natanz, Isfahan, and Arak alone would stretch Israel's capabilities, and planners might be reluctant to enlarge the raid further.[2]

Israel is capable of carrying out these attacks on its own. Its F-16 and F-15 aircraft, equipped with conformal fuel tanks and refueled with 707-based and KC-130 tankers toward the beginning and end of the attack planes' flight profiles, have the range to reach the target set, deliver their payloads in the face of Iranian air defenses, and return to their bases. The disclosure of Israeli acquisition of Boeing 777-sized unmanned aerial vehicles might offer Israel expanded attack options. The munitions necessary to penetrate the targets are currently in Israel's inventory in sufficient numbers; they include Bomb Live Unit (BLU)-109 and BLU-113 bombs that carry 2,000 and 5,000 pounds, respectively, of high-energy explosives. These GPS-guided weapons are extremely accurate and can be lofted from attacking aircraft 15 kilometers from their target, thereby reducing the attackers' need to fly through air defenses. Israel also has a laser-guided version of these bombs that is more accurate than the GPS variant and could covertly deploy a special-operations laser designation unit to illuminate aim points (the Israelis reportedly did this for the attack on the al-Kibar facility in Syria).

These munitions could be expected to damage the targets severely. Natanz is the only one of the three likely targets that is largely underground, sheltered by up to

23 meters of soil and concrete. BLU-type bombs used in a "burrowing" mode, however, could penetrate deeply enough to fragment the inner surface of the ceiling structures above the highly fragile centrifuge arrays and even precipitate the collapse of the entire structure. Burrowing requires that attacking aircraft deliver their second and third bombs into the cavity created by the first. GPS-guided munitions are accurate enough to do this in just under one out of every two attempts. So the use of three bombs per aim point would confer better than a 70 percent probability of success. (Laser-guided munitions

are more capable of a successful burrow on the first try.) The uranium conversion facility in Isfahan and reactor at Arak are not buried and could be heavily damaged, or completely destroyed. This would be possible even if Iran managed to down a third of the Israeli strike package, a feat that would far exceed historical ratios of bomber losses by any country in any previous war.

Such relatively favorable ballistic assessments do not mean that the mission as a whole would be easy. On the contrary, a coordinated air attack would be complicated and highly risky. The three plausible routes to Iran involve overflight of third countries: the northern approach would likely follow the Syrian-Turkish border and risk violation of Turkey's airspace; the central flight path would cross Jordan and Iraq; a southern route would transit the lower end of Jordan, Saudi Arabia, and possibly Kuwait. All but two of these countries are, to a greater or lesser degree, hostile to Israel. The exceptions, Jordan and Turkey, would not wish their airspace to be used for an Israeli attack. Turkey in October 2009 canceled an annual trilateral exercise involving Israel, a possible indicator of how Ankara might react to an Israeli violation of its airspace. In any event, overflight would jeopardize Israeli diplomatic relations with both countries. With respect to Syria and Saudi Arabia, operational concerns would trump diplomatic ones. If either country detects Israeli aircraft and chooses to challenge the overflight using surface-to-air missiles or intercepting aircraft, Israel's intricate attack plan could well be derailed.

Overflight of Iraq, whose airspace is under de facto U.S. control, would also be diplomatically awkward for Israel and would risk a deadly clash with American air defenses because the intruding aircraft would not have the appropriate identification, friend or foe (IFF) codes. Israel would have to carefully weigh the operational risk and most of all the cost of a strike to its most vital bilateral relationship, especially if President Obama had explicitly asked Prime Minister Netanyahu not to order an attack.

The sheer distances involved pose a challenge as well. The targets lie at the outermost 1,750-kilometer range limits of Israeli tactical aircraft. Diplomatic and military factors would confine Israeli refueling operations to international airspace where tankers can orbit safely for long periods. These locations, while usable, are suboptimal. They would yield the attackers little leeway to loiter in their target areas or engage in the fuel-intensive maneuvering typical of dogfights and evasion of surface-to-air missiles. The limited number of tankers would limit the number of sorties.

Israel could time the attacks with the aim of minimizing Iranian casualties. There is no time of day or night, however, when these facilities are likely to be completely empty of people. Moreover, a stray bomb—whether the result of guidance error, faulty intelligence, or the location of nuclear facilities amid the civilian population—cannot be excluded. Civilian casualties in the hundreds are possible if not likely.

A final consideration for Israeli planners would be the effect of explosives on the nuclear materials stored at the uranium conversion facility at Isfahan and the enrichment facility at Natanz. Both facilities are likely to contain uranium hexafluoride, and Natanz produces low-enriched uranium. Although these materials are not radioactive and do not pose radiological risks, the release of uranium into the environment would almost certainly raise public health concerns due to fine airborne debris and the inevitable propaganda exploitation that would follow.

This combination of diplomatic and operational complexities would clearly give Israeli leaders pause. To act, they would have to perceive a grave threat to the state of Israel and no reliable alternative for eliminating that threat.

"There is a difference in the way the world looks when you are looking through the sight of a weapon and when you are looking into the barrel of a weapon," said Shlomo Brom, a retired IDF brigadier general and former deputy national security adviser in summer 2009. "When you are looking through the sight you ask, 'What if I miss?'" When looking through the barrel, the main question is, '"what will happen if he hits me?'" Brom, when we met with him in Tel Aviv, was no great advocate of military action, but he did warn against assuming that Israel would decide against attacking because the costs are too high or the payoff insufficient. From the Israeli perspective, he said, it is true that uncertainties are many, including the possibility of unknown facilities and very rapid reconstruction. "But on the Iranian side, they can't be certain that [the attacker] doesn't know all these things, and won't bomb them over and over."[3]

The likelihood of Israel deciding to attack depends on Israeli assessments of U.S. and international resolve to block Iran's pursuit of a nuclear weapons capability; the state of the Iranian program; the amount of time a successful strike would buy to be worth the expected risks and costs (a point on which there is a spectrum of Israeli views, from six months to five years); whether Israel believes there is a clandestine Iranian program, which would lead some Israelis to conclude that an attack would buy no time at all; and the effect of a strike on the U.S.-Israel relationship. Because none of these factors is constant, estimates about the likelihood of an Israeli strike will vary.

It is clear, however, that Israel sees the stakes as very high. Netanyahu's UN General Assembly speech of September 2009 emphasized the existential nature of the threat that he and others in the current government believe Iran represents.[4] His emphasis on the Holocaust as a defining feature of Jewish history and his apparent self-conception as the one who bears the burden of preventing yet another such disaster suggest that U.S. calculations of risk and benefit that tilt toward Israeli restraint might prove to be mirror-imaging of a particularly deceptive sort.

"The Israeli leader of the moment would agonize over his historical duty," said Ariel Levite, former Israeli national security adviser and former deputy director general in Israel's Atomic Energy Commission. "For Begin [regarding the 1981 attack at Osirak] it was between him and God. There is strong evidence that that's how Bibi [Netanyahu] defines his historical mission."[5] In this regard, a Netanyahu adviser's report that the prime minister looks at Iran as a modern-day reincarnation of the Amalekites is striking.[6] In the Hebrew Bible, the Amalekites were a predatory Canaanite tribe that victimized the weak and infirm among the Israelites who were making their way to the Promised Land. God commands the Israelites to annihilate the Amalekites and destroy their property. When, at a later period, King Saul fails to comply with this instruction, his crown is given over to his rival David. Without wading too deep into psychological waters, Netanyahu's use of this ancient trope probably reveals something of his view of Iran, his duty to stave off the threat, and the consequences of failure to fulfill that duty. Even setting aside this speculative mind-reading, Netanyahu's articulation of these themes could make it more difficult for him to explain a decision not to use force later, in the event that diplomacy fails and Iran's program progresses.

Israeli officials are aware that no conceivable Israeli strike could completely eliminate Iran's nuclear threat and that an attack might only intensify longer-term risks as Iran reconstituted covertly. But some of them advance an argument long made by counterterrorism officials in a different context: any effort to counter Iran's nuclear challenge is going to be like "mowing the lawn." Just as the grass will grow again, so will the nuclear program; Israel will just have to mow again. And as Iran's reconstitution effort goes underground and its defenses are enhanced, Israel's intelligence and military capabilities will have to keep pace.

They also argue, however, that the advantages of buying time should not be discounted. The 1981 Osirak attack won two crucial decades during which Operation Desert Storm effectively disarmed Iraq and Operation Iraqi Freedom finally decapitated it. Neither tectonic event could have been predicted in 1981. (The counterargument is that the Osirak raid stimulated Iraq to switch to a highly enriched uranium [HEU] route and vastly increased the money and manpower devoted to the program.[7] But whether or not the bombing set back Iraq's program, the important point is that many Israelis believe that it did.) On this Israeli view, a strike might prove worthwhile in ways that neither Israel nor the United States can anticipate at this stage.

War, Peace, and Linkage

While U.S. officials—including the president—have declared a nuclear armed Iran to be "unacceptable," the administration has been clear in wanting to prevent such an outcome through peaceful diplomatic means. Without forswearing the eventual use of military force, senior U.S. officials have also indicated that a preventive strike on Iran by Israel would be "ill advised," "very destabilizing," and "likely very bad," and thus not in the U.S. interest.[8] These concerns have evidently been transmitted privately to the Israeli government.

The prospect of an open breach between Washington and Jerusalem is worrying to both sides. After what looked like steady convergence during the Bush administration, the first year of the Obama administration indicated a phase of counter-cycle in the two allies' politics and strategic thinking. The new, liberal American president considered the Bush legacy in the Middle East to be a disaster, and was ambitious to set a new course. The new, conservative Israeli government expressed its wariness of a new president whom Israelis suspected of lacking the pro-Israel reflexes of his predecessor. From the outset, mutual distrust was evident in a complex, sometimes muted but clearly anxious argument about the linkage between Iran's nuclear threat and broader problems of war and peace in the Middle East.

The term *linkage*, as U.S. and Israeli government officials and commentators have used it, is freighted. The concept lay at the center of the Nixon administration's policy, almost 40 years ago, toward the Soviet Union; it was contentious even then. As Henry Kissinger used the term, it meant that the Soviets would not get political concessions from the United States on things the Kremlin wanted, such as arms control negotiations, while the Soviets were supporting U.S. enemies on Vietnamese battlefields. Linkage was thought of in bargaining terms, rather than in a causal or correlative sense. This straightforward exchange of concessions, which intended to leave each side better off, at least in its own estimation, proved to be even more controversial than Nixon and Kissinger anticipated. Arms control advocates saw negotiations over strategic arms limitations as an intrinsic good, partly because they viewed a world with fewer nuclear weapons as a safer one and partly because arms talks gave antagonistic super-powers a pretext for bilateral diplomacy, which advocates saw as an inherently beneficial, even if contact led to no serious compromises by either side. Thus, for the arms control lobby within and outside of government, linkage was a bad idea. On the right, linkage was condemned as a reward for Soviet restraint that should have been exer-cised in the first place. The corollary to this was the belief that linkage would encourage the Soviets to take aggres-sive actions solely for the purpose of extorting conces-sions from Washington.

Echoes of the angry, partisan American debate over linkage in the period 1969–1974 can be heard in the current multilayered dispute about the nexus between Iran's nuclear threat and the Arab-Israeli peace process. Clashing interpretations of linkage emerged at the first meeting between President Obama and Prime Minister Netanyahu, who formulated their conceptions of link-age in precisely reciprocal terms. For Obama, there are "Arab states in the region—the Jordanians, the Egyp-tians, the Saudis—who...share concerns about Iran's potential development of nuclear weapons. In order for us to potentially realign interests in the region in a constructive way, bolstering...the Palestinian-Israeli peace track is critical." He expanded on this comment in response to a subsequent question, which paraphrased Netanyahu government claims that "only if the Iranian threat will be solved...can [Israel] achieve real progress on the Palestinian threat." Obama acknowledged that the threat of a nuclear-armed Iran would "give any leader of any country pause..." but continued, "having said that, if there is a linkage between Iran and the Israeli-Palestinian peace process, I personally believe it actually runs the other way. To the extent we can make peace with the Palestinians—between the Palestinians and the Israelis, then I actually think it strengthens our hand in the international community in dealing with a potential Iranian threat."[9] This was not linkage in a strictly Kissingerian sense, in that Obama did not say that the United States would curtail its efforts to mobilize a coalition against Iran if Israel dragged its feet on peace talks with Palestinians. But it does put the onus on the Jewish state by implying that Israel's inability to move forward on its Palestinian front would hamstring Washington's diplomatic effort to disarm Iran.

As the reporter's question at the press conference indicated, Netanyahu had been pressing the reverse of this linkage to set the stage for his visit to Washington. Pointing to Iran's broad regional offensive, particularly its support for Hamas and Hezbollah, he and his aides argued that progress in the peace process would be impossible until Iran had been contained. Iran was empowering rejectionists and undermining moderates; under these conditions, pursuing negotiations with Palestinians was like trying to shingle a roof in a hurricane. If Israel were to take the risks involved in going back to the table, the United States would have to take tangible steps to rein in Iran, particularly its nuclear ambitions, which raised the specter of nuclear weapons transferred to atavistic Palestinians emboldened by their patron's defiance of the United States. As with Washington's position, this was hard linkage, even if it was not quite as explicit as the classic formula.[10]

A simple and literal concept of linkage between Iran's nuclear program and the Israeli-Palestinian peace process is difficult to sustain. Netanyahu's version misses the forest for the trees. It is true that Iran supports the spoilers in the peace process, Hamas and Hezbollah. Tehran generously funds both movements and supplies them with arms.[11] Weapons captured by Israel Defense Force units in Lebanon in 2006 bore Iranian markings, and both the United States and UNIFIL II, the United Nations force in southern Lebanon, have alleged large transfers of missiles, heavy weapons, and munitions to Hezbollah via Syria over the years. Israel has intercepted sizable maritime arms shipments destined for Palestinians as well. The extravagant publicity Israeli authorities have orchestrated for these interdicted shipments has raised suspicions that they were staged by Israel to discredit Iran, but there is no evidence to support such skepticism. Tehran has been caught red-handed more than once.[12]

Hezbollah, however, is not an insurmountable obstacle to Israeli-Palestinian peace. Although Hezbollah provocations could disrupt Israeli-Palestinian negotiations and erode Israeli confidence in Arab intentions, much as Hamas attacks scuttled Shimon Peres's government and undercut the peace process in 1995–1996, its ability to do so is limited. Israel, at any rate, has acted as though it views the Lebanon conflict as separable from the Palestinian problem. It was the current Israeli minister of defense, Ehud Barak, who decided that Israel should unilaterally withdraw from Lebanon and disengage from what had become a pointless war of attrition with Hezbollah. By withdrawing, Israel was implicitly conceding that southern Lebanon was no longer relevant to other more pressing geostrategic concerns, including its occupation of the West Bank and Gaza.

Hamas poses a different problem, and Iranian support does strengthen its position in Gaza. Tehran's patronage is one of several factors that discourages Fatah from taking the risks entailed in forming the unity government with Hamas that would presumably be necessary before productive talks with Israel could begin. Yet Hamas was radical before Iran saw an opportunity for meddling, while Iranian assistance was of no avail when the IDF entered Gaza in 2008 to put an end to rocket launches aimed at cities in southern Israel. In any case, the militants' popularity, according to polling in late 2009, is lower than at any time since their 2006 election victory both in Gaza and West Bank, a trend that has probably been accelerated by most Palestinians' distaste for Hamas's flirtation with a Shi'a foreign power.[13]

The case for linkage that Obama made was premised on the idea that resolution of the Arab-Israeli conflict on equitable terms would be the key to fixing the region's other problems. His national security advisor, General James Jones, advanced this proposition in his keynote address to the 2009 conference sponsored by J Street, a new, progressive Jewish lobby: "If there was one problem I could recommend to the President, if he could solve one problem, this would be it." Jones went on to explain that an Israeli-Palestinian peace agreement would create "ripples" around the world. "The reverse is not true. This is the epicenter."[14] Democratic administrations are not uniquely susceptible to this idea. The first Bush administration perceived this linkage, but saw it running in different directions at different times. Before Operation Desert Storm, they believed that the elimination of Iraq as "the last radical alternative in the Middle East"[15] would isolate Palestinian rejectionists and ripen the moment for an Arab-Israeli peace. The road to Jerusalem went through Baghdad. After the war, the push for an Arab-Israeli agreement at Madrid, preceded by serious pressure on the Shamir government in

Israel, would pave the way for Arab acquiescence in a massive regional expansion of U.S. military bases and Arab concurrence in an ambitious nonproliferation scheme. At that point, the road to Riyadh went through Jerusalem. The second Bush administration initiated the Annapolis talks in 2007 because it was thought that regional support for the precarious U.S. position in Iraq could be secured through a simulacrum of progress in Israeli-Palestinian talks. Thus the road to Baghdad traversed Jerusalem.

In truth, although the many serious problems of the Middle Eastern political order are no doubt interrelated, it would be facile to imagine that they are linked in some Newtonian fashion, such that a final status accord between Israelis and Palestinians would solve them. The clash in Kirkuk between expansionist Kurdish ambitions and Sunni nationalism, while Iraq's largely Shi'a army keeps an uneasy peace; incipient civil war in Yemen; Iranian territorial claims in the Persian Gulf; economic meltdown in Dubai, a growing demographic challenge in the Gulf Cooperation Council states; sectarian deadlock in Lebanon; growth of Muslim Brotherhood networks in Jordan and Egypt—these are just a few examples of problems that would not be solved by a settlement of Palestinian and Israeli claims.

Arab leaders generally make national security decisions on the basis of their perceptions of the threat to their regime or state.[16] Washington, for example, made its big breakthrough in persuading GCC states to provide access for U.S. military forces just when Israel had invaded Lebanon, laid siege to Beirut and forced Yasir Arafat's flight to Tunis in 1982. The looming threat of a mobilized, revolutionary Iran far outweighed anxieties about a grave setback to Palestinian national aspirations. A more dramatic case was the decision of the al-Saud to host U.S. forces in preparation for the invasion of Kuwait in 1991. The fact that Israel had just suppressed the first Palestinian intifada without any meaningful concessions toward Palestinian autonomy did not deter the Saudi ruling family from its decision. The question for them was not how their subjects would perceive the arrival of an enormous army deployed by Israel's chief ally and patron; rather, it was whether the al Saud would prefer the decidedly inferior option of ruling their kingdom from "...hotel rooms in Cairo and Paris and London."[17] The essence of decision making by Arab states regarding the standoff between America and Iran is likely to be similar to the way Washington makes such decisions. The United States routinely works on an intimate basis with countries that do not recognize Israel, propagate global media messages incompatible with U.S. values, and discriminate against Christians, Jews, and women. Congress and public interest groups frequently complain about these bilateral relationships, but in matters of strategic interest, their qualms are disregarded by decision makers. And so it is with Middle Eastern governments. Public opinion is taken into account, but only up to a point.

On balance, the feasibility of hard linkage between Israeli policy toward Palestinians and the challenge posed by Iran seems questionable. Returning to Henry Kissinger's experiment with linkage for a moment, it is worth looking at his own explanation for the failure of his initial attempt to link U.S. agreement to strategic arms limitation talks and Soviet cooperation on Vietnam: "The two issues were too incommensurable; the outcome of the strategic arms discussion was too uncertain, the Hanoi leadership was too intractable, and the time scale required for either negotiation too difficult to synchronize."[18]

Yet although hard linkage may be difficult, or even impossible, to establish, there is nonetheless an indirect linkage at work. At the most obvious level, this might be thought of as the connection between U.S. interests in the Middle East and Arab perceptions of American engagement on behalf of Palestinians. It would be naive to imagine that such perceptions would transform U.S. fortunes in the region and certainly not overnight. But as a way to reduce resistance to other forms of U.S. influence and reduce barriers to Washington's message on other issues—including Iran's nuclear ambitions—bold but careful intervention to pave the way for a Palestinian state would be hard to beat.

There are four basic reasons why a credible, foreseeable end to Israel's occupation over Palestinians would serve important American purposes. First, it is simply difficult to swim in a sea of Arab ill will. The Palestinians' plight is a powerful emotive issue across the Arab world, and American responsibility for the behavior of its Israeli ally is assumed. Over the decades, some of the American discourse on this matter has revealed a temptation to believe that Israel's rule over the Palestinians is, in the grand scheme of things, limited in its importance. This illusion springs from a kernel of truth. For half a century Arab regimes, all undemocratic and many despotic, have stoked up hatred of Israel in order to deflect attention from their own misrule. Their "support" for the Palestinians has been belied by repeated betrayals. Outrage at Israeli human-rights abuses has been hypocritical, given the silence about the truly psychopathic cruelties inflicted by Saddam Hussein, Hafez al-Assad, Muammar Gadhafi, and others. That the outrage is selective, though, makes it no less real. It is utopian to imagine that Arab populations will be enraged about Arabs repressing and killing Arabs as they are about Israeli Jews repressing and (far more rarely) killing Arabs. This is a cultural reality, created by Arab ethnocentrism (and compounded, perhaps, by less excusable anti-Semitism), which the United States will have to address as a strategic reality. The larger strategic reality is that the United States needs a settlement of the Israel—Palestine conflict that Arabs in general eventually come to recognize as just.

Second, the prestige and regional influence that Iran derives from its murderous rejection of Israel is, to some significant degree, a function of Israel's visible mistreatment of Palestinians. Many thoughtful Israelis understand this. David Menashri, an Iranian-born Israeli professor at Tel Aviv University, has argued: "Instead of threatening to bomb [Iran], we should work on the Palestinian peace process. It would be good for us anyway, and it would weaken Iran as a bonus."[19] The logic of this argument can be found in the question: if Iran did not have the emotive issue of Israel-Palestine, would it have any appeal to the Arab world whatsoever? "Not a hell of a lot," answers Ray Takeyh, a leading Iran expert in the United States. "Its role in Lebanese politics"—through its sponsorship of Hezbollah—"would continue." And it could continue its effort to promote Shi'a solidarity throughout the Middle East. "But in terms of pan-Arab opinion, the Israel-Palestine problem is very helpful to Tehran."[20]

Third, Palestinian suffering is a powerful propaganda weapon and recruiting tool for al-Qaeda's war against the United States. This should not really be a controversial point, yet it is readily distorted by polemicists of both right and left. To be clear: Osama bin Laden's war against America was not principally motivated by the plight of the Palestinians. When he did take up their cause, moreover, his pronouncements made absolutely clear that he was unconcerned about where the ultimate border dividing Israel from Palestine might be set. The answer to injustice, in al-Qaeda's book, is the destruction of Israel. This is also the long-held view of those groups, such as Hamas and Palestinian Islamic Jihad, which are indeed directly concerned with Israel. Moreover, their behavior has repeated a familiar dynamic of terrorism— whereby it intensifies whenever compromise seems near. So America's problem—and indeed, Israel's problem— with Islamist terrorism is not going to vanish on the day that a sovereign Palestinian state comes into being. Yet the tide of Arab anger—and more broadly, Islamic anger—can be reduced, and this will have an effect on terrorism's attractiveness. "It [the Palestinian issue] is a potent element in the single narrative and the one that has the greatest durability in attracting recruits to the jihadist cause," argues Nigel Inkster, former second in command and director of operations and intelligence in the British Secret Intelligence Service. Inkster goes on to note that, although other causes—the wars in Iraq and Afghanistan, the perfidy of Arab regimes—will ebb and flow in the Islamist imagination, Palestine "is something to which jihadist propagandists can always default." And there is an all-too-human reason for this: above such issues as democracy, the "concept of justice is something that resonates very powerfully in the Arab world."[21]

The Definition of Threat

The fourth reason is probably the most important one. It is a deep and abiding American interest to support an Israeli state that is secure, democratic, and Jewish, and this interest—shared, obviously, by Israel itself—is threatened by the stalemate over Palestine.

It is understandable that many Israelis interpret Palestinian radicalism as an *epiphenomenon*—to borrow Matthew Yglesias's term—of the more significant confrontation with Iran and the Islamist radicalism that is exploited and sometimes directed by it.[22] It is understandable but dangerously misguided, because the decades-long humiliation of Palestinians under Israeli occupation is a strategic factor and long-term threat that exists entirely apart from what Iran or al Qaeda may do or say. Successive Israeli governments were encouraged and abetted in discounting this threat by a Bush administration that—although officially and, in the case of President Bush himself, sincerely committed to Palestinian statehood—was utterly unrealistic in requiring a complete transformation of Palestinian attitudes and ideology before requiring Israel to fulfill its commitments. (This was one of the crippling distortions that President Bush's outlandish concept of the "war on terrorism" inflicted on U.S. policy and strategy.)

Fear of the Iranian nuclear threat interacts with the stalemate over Palestine in ways that could compound the dysfunction of Israeli politics. Indeed, when some Israelis speak of the existential threat posed by a nuclear Iran, they mean something more complicated than an unprovoked nuclear attack from the Islamic Republic. They fear that under the shadow of a nuclear Iran, Israel will suffer an inexorable and terminal loss of national nerve. The country's best brains will drain into the Western diaspora. In this scenario, those who remain—disproportionately Sephardic, Russian, or religious—will fuel a politics increasingly characterized by intransigence over Palestine and a reliance on the use of force that would jeopardize the country's long-term national interests.

The circumstances of Israel's most recent wars lend support to this thesis. The Lebanon and Gaza wars were humanitarian catastrophes for the local Arabs and propaganda disasters for Israel and the United States. They were meant to restore the prestige and credibility of Israeli deterrent capabilities, which were thought to have been weakened by attacks that followed Israel's withdrawal from both Lebanon and Gaza.[23] Israel's conduct of both wars, which punished civilians heavily, suggests that it is losing its strategic perspective along with its national confidence in nonmilitary solutions to security challenges.

That is not, however, the lesson that most Israelis have drawn. There is in Israel a burgeoning confidence in the use of force and deployment of physical defenses. The breast-beating that followed the awkward war against Hezbollah in the summer of 2006 and bloody Gaza offensive in the winter of 2008–2009 has given way to a conviction that these campaigns were effective. As of January 2010, there have been virtually no rocket launches from either Lebanon or Gaza and neither Hamas nor Hezbollah has attempted to ambush Israelis. From this perspective, Israelis resigned to indefinite policing of Palestinian territory absent a political settlement feel up to the task; moreover, assiduous analysis of tactical, doctrinal, and other defects that plagued IDF operations in Lebanon, combined with an exerted effort to remedy them, has left Israelis comfortable with the thought of a second round.

To these hardened Israeli attitudes must be added the baleful influence of the settlers' movement. Most of the 300,000 settlers in the occupied West Bank have scant concern about the viability of a two-state solution. These are active agents of Palestinians' humiliation, and though their attitudes may not inspire admiration among the

Israeli majority, they appear to have a stranglehold on Israel's political fate. Their fanaticism echoes the Islamist zealotry of Iran's ruling clerics and of Hamas. It was in the fanatical devotion to God, for example, that Israeli law student Yigal Amir assassinated Prime Minister Yitzhak Rabin. Amir believed that his act had been sanctioned by a religious ruling. In being prepared to hand over sacred Jewish land to Palestinians, Rabin was judged to be endangering the redemption of the Jewish people as a whole. Sacred claims that purport to channel God's will are, by definition, nonnegotiable. They will pit zealous Jewish Israelis against zealous Palestinians as embodied by Hamas, and will sustain and renourish the mythology of undying enmity.

That the feasibility of a two-state settlement with the Palestinians is slipping disastrously away constitutes the most obvious threat to Israel's future as a state that is both Jewish and democratic. Israel's Prime Minister Ehud Olmert, just before leaving office, was among the latest to voice the blinding truth that active politicians find difficult to utter: "If the day comes when the two-state solution collapses, and we face a South African-style struggle for equal voting rights...then, as soon as that happens, the State of Israel is finished."[24] Olmert's mentor, the relentlessly hard-line Ariel Sharon, came to the same conclusion in 2003; he spoke of Israel's need to "sever" itself from the Palestinians and he formed the new centrist party, Kadima, as a vehicle to do so. In January 2010, Labor politician and former prime minister Ehud Barak, who had joined the Netanyahu government as defense minister, echoed Olmert in warning that conditions of "apartheid" were the only alternative to the two states.[25]

The shape of a two-state solution is well known. It entails substantial Israeli withdrawal from the occupied territories, including dismantlement of many settlements; equitable swaps of land to compensate for wherever the final borders deviate from the 1967 "Green Line;" some form of shared sovereignty over Jerusalem; effective outside security commitments against terrorism; and a strict limit on refugee returns to Israel proper in order to preserve the Jewish character of the Israeli state. In other words, there is a general understanding that the eventual settlement will look a great deal like the one put forward at Camp David, and revised at Taba, under the auspices of the Clinton administration.

Versions of a two-state solution are nearly as old as the conflict itself. The Peel Commission endorsed it in 1937, and in 1947 the UN enshrined it in the original plan for partitioning Palestine. But alternatives to the two-state solution are also as old as the Arab-Israeli conflict. The Arabs attempted to implement a one-state solution in 1948 by waging war against the newly declared Israel (although historians have questioned the determination, let alone capacity, of Arab governments to push the Jews into the sea).[26] In the run-up to the Six-Day War of June 1967, Egypt's Gamal Abdel Nasser may or may not have been bluffing, but his speeches were unambiguous challenges to Israel's existence.[27] Israel, in any event, called the bluff and triumphed spectacularly. Subsequent strategies of Palestinian resistance and Israeli occupation could not have been better designed to render a two-state settlement unviable. The terrorist mode of resistance to Israel's occupation had profound effects on Israelis' willingness to trust the Palestinians as a negotiating partner. Palestinian terrorism gathered momentum with the spectacular hijackings and blowing up of Swiss, British, and American airliners in Jordan in 1970, the kidnapping and murder of 11 Israeli athletes at the 1972 Munich Olympics, the kidnapping of 90 Israeli schoolchildren at Ma'alot in 1974 (20 died in the rescue attempt), and the hijacking of an Air France flight to Entebbe, Uganda, in 1976. After Israel did undertake, from the Israelis' perspective, a tremendous leap of faith—in the Oslo process, and at Camp David and Taba—the subsequent waves of suicide bombings were deeply traumatic in their effect on Israelis' readiness to take a comparable leap of faith again. Yet the Palestinians too have had tangible reasons to doubt Israel's intentions. Israel's government did inform the United States, after its 1967 victory, that Israel wanted formal peace—that is, formal recognition, finally, from the Arabs—and some border modifications to ensure security, but that it was prepared to concede the return of most captured territory. But it also embarked on policies that progressively undermined the prospects of such an agreement. The Israelis started constructing settlements in the Golan Heights, West Bank, Gaza, and Sinai—originally for strategic reasons but soon taking on ideological and religious fervor, especially under the Likud government of Menachem Begin, which replaced Labour in 1977. The settlements policy was a historic mistake. That Israel had felt itself cornered into the Six-Day War did not relieve it of responsibility for thinking about the consequences of its new power over Palestinians whom it would not—and could not—expel or offer citizenship. Even though most of the Arabs were refusing to negotiate in the 1970s and 1980s, enlightened self-interest should have led Israel to better prepare for the peace deal that would one day have to be negotiated. With the continuation of settlement activity under successive Israeli governments, it could be argued that Israel has made its own attempt to impose a one-state solution.

Alternatives to two states, once discredited by military or political failure, are now discussed openly, with either a more-in-sorrow-than-in-anger sense of anguish, or a smug sense of I-told-you-so. In the latter camp are those on the fringe who have long pressed the case for a binational state encompassing Israel, the West Bank and Gaza, which, given demographic realities, would swiftly cease to be a Jewish state. The former group of lapsed two-state proponents is the more worrying bellwether.[28] They point to a dismal accumulation of facts on the ground. There is a widening gap between the maximum Israel will offer in terms of territory and what Palestinians say they will accept,[29] and a generalized sense on both sides of the line that the other party is unprepared to make necessary compromises (despite abundant polling data indicating that Palestinian and Israeli publics desire an agreement that will leave them in peace).[30] Israeli infrastructure on the West Bank, especially settlement construction, has grown significantly since the Oslo accord in 1993, subsequent implementation agreements, and the "road map" accepted by both sides in 2003;[31] it will be difficult to dismantle. Israeli political leadership, generally weak, is rendered nearly impotent by a flawed constitution and dysfunctional multiparty political structure, in which the compromises required to form governments almost invariably rule out adequate compromise with the Palestinians.[32] A sharp swing to the right in Israeli politics both reflects and worsens the stalemate. In early 2009, the Labor Party imploded at the polls. Kadima, the centrist party created by Ariel Sharon and led by former Likudniks Ehud Olmert and Tzipi Livni, won a plurality of the vote but could not form a government. Kadima, which led the country into the 2006 war in Lebanon, was held responsible for its messy and inconclusive results, which were attributed to the government's unpreparedness for the war and its subsequent unwillingness, in the electorate's view, to fight to the finish. Netanyahu was the beneficiary of this dissatisfaction, having hammered on these points throughout the military campaign and again, two and half years later, during the election campaign.

Then there are the Palestinians. The quip, attributed to Abba Eban, Israel's foreign minister from 1966 to 1974, that the Arabs "never miss an opportunity to miss an opportunity," seemed to be borne out spectacularly by Arafat's failure in 2000, at Camp David and then Taba, to grasp then-Israeli prime minister Ehud Barak's offer of a Palestinian state—or at least to make a credible counterproposal. The unleashing of the second intifada, soon accompanied by suicide terrorism, may or may not have been outside of Arafat's control, but it proved disastrous for efforts to resume constructive negotiations. To be sure, a school of Camp David revisionism has made a credible case that the story of Camp David's failure was more complicated than originally presented: during Oslo years of the 1990s, Palestinians had ample reason to distrust the Israelis, having experienced the hemming in, through settlements and checkpoints, of Palestinian "Bantustans"; in this context, Barak's offer did not look all that brilliant.[33] Still, there has been a frustrating and enduring failure on the part of Palestinians to negotiate strategically and in a spirit of realism; they constantly assert "rights" and "justice" to the detriment of assessing their bargaining position and looking for negotiable common ground. Prospects for resumption of meaningful negotiations have been further dimmed, of course, by the violent fragmentation of Palestinian politics, the rise of Hamas, its victory in parliamentary elections, and the near civil war resulting in Hamas's takeover of Gaza.

Perhaps the most forbidding barrier to a two-state compromise is the renewed demand of each party for explicit acceptance of its narrative by the other side as the necessary condition for peace. It is as though the vast ocean of political, security, and other technical issues that have been negotiated on and off since 1993 has receded, stranding the parties' ancient core claims on the beach, like the wreck of a long lost vessel. As Netanyahu expressed the demand, "We want them [the Palestinians] to say the simplest things, to our people and to their people. This will then open the door to solving other problems, no matter how difficult. The fundamental condition for ending the conflict is the public, binding and sincere Palestinian recognition of Israel as the national homeland of the Jewish People."[34] Palestinian demands, on the other hand, reemphasize the right of refugee return to territory that constituted Palestine before the establishment of the State of Israel. For Israelis, this is tantamount to a demand that they acknowledge original sin: that the foundation of their state was a monstrous injustice, which robbed Palestinians of their homeland. For Palestinians, recognition of Israel would be to deny the justice of their claim and renounce the right to their patrimony. As Robert Malley and Hussein Agha have observed, these positions relocate the conflict from 1967 and the status of the West Bank and Gaza to 1948 and the status of a Jewish state. Accordingly, "a two-state solution might end the occupation, but will not end the conflict." It is hard to see what sort of negotiation can emerge from this existential knife fight.[35]

Does Time Always Heal?

To its many skeptics, the Obama administration's renewed push for an Israel-Palestine final settlement is the classic triumph of hope over experience. Why, the skeptics ask, should yet another iteration of the hoary "peace process" yield any better results?

The not-so-bright prospects for a full and final settlement have stimulated some thinking about alternatives. Some speak of resurrecting the so-called Jordanian option, which would return much of the West Bank to Jordanian administration.[36] The Netanyahu government has argued that economic, civil, and security development of the West Bank is more plausible and should take precedence over formal negotiations. Some Palestinians also see advantages, or at least no penalties, in the deferral or even demise of the two-state option. From their perspective, Israel is not going to permit a fully sovereign Palestinian state, so there is little advantage in pursuing an agreement.[37] Given this reality, a truce arrangement that minimizes violent contact with Israel, preserves the flow of international aid and boosts economic performance and job creation, and offers significant propaganda opportunities is the superior course. On this view, the long-run prospects for a demographic victory take on a special significance (though the mechanism by which differential fertility rates might secure a triumphant state for Palestinians residing in the territories are not direct or obvious). Because the respective narratives appear incompatible, the idea of an interim but long-term "truce" attracts the adherence of some strange bedfellows: Israelis who say that nothing is possible until Palestinians come to terms with the idea of a Jewish state in Palestine; members of Hamas who agree that this is the insurmountable problem, but also suggest that a decades-long truce, or *Hudna*, might be possible until one side, or both, changes its mind.[38]

But if there is a case to be made against peacemakers continuing to knock their heads against unyielding walls, there is an equally compelling need to recognize that the passage of time has rarely, if ever, worked to the advantage of peace and reconciliation between Israeli Jews and Palestinian Arabs. An Israeli occupation spanning generations has not bred Palestinian moderation. Whereas Israel once had to contend with a radical, terrorist, but secular PLO, it now faces a radical, terrorist and deeply religious Hamas. Indeed, the *reductio ad absurdum* of the wait-for-something-better strategy can be seen in the "West Bank First" policy—whereby Fatah-controlled West Bank was to be supported politically and with generous aid, whereas Hamas-controlled Gaza would be subjected to a blockade. The policy has been supported, at least implicitly, by the Quartet of the United States, EU, UN, and Russia. Its operating theory—that collective punishment would render Gazans, who could see the benefits for their West Bank brethren, more moderate—was ludicrous on its face and has not, in any event, been vindicated.

To the effects of time must be added the effects of a possible war with Iran. Some supporters of military action against Iran will also argue that the effect on the peace process would be neutral or even positive. There are some limited precedents in the Middle East to support this argument. The case was made in chapter 1, for example, that Saddam Hussein's defeat in 1991 imparted momentum to the Oslo process. Looking at the Arab side, Henry Kissinger drew on his experience in 1973 to argue that Egyptian President Anwar Sadat launched the October War against Israel not to win back territory, but to create a psychological shock that would make both Arabs and Israelis more serious about seeking peace. It was, according to Kissinger, an extremely rare case of a statesman who fought a war "to lay the basis for moderation in its aftermath"—and it worked.[39]

Similar happy results from air strikes against Iran—even if they lead to a wider war implicating the United States—cannot be ruled out. Iran's prestige could be usefully tarnished. Fearful Arab regimes might be secretly or openly gratified. The Iranian regime—already fragile—might even fall to a Green movement eager to end Iran's international isolation.

All of these consequences are possible. They are not, however, predictable. It is worth remembering, in this regard, the predictions of a positive, democratizing, regional domino effect that supporters of the Iraq war made for it in 2003. Some of those same supporters now claim vindication in the fact that Iraq in early 2010 is far more peaceful than the Iraq that was sinking into civil war in 2006. This is true enough, just as it is also true that the removal of Saddam Hussein was a great benefit to the Iraqi people and the wider world. Of course, things were likely to get better sometime. Meanwhile, the carnage and chaos was immense, and the costs—in Iraqi, American, and other coalition lives, treasure, American prestige, and Arab and Islamic anger—have been huge.

A war launched by Israel against Iran might have similar strategic costs. Rallying millions of Muslims, whether Sunni or Shi'ite, to the Iranian cause could revive the specter of a civilizational war between Islam and the West, inspire fresh recruits to global terrorism, draw in Arab states both allied with and against Iran, and doom Obama's initiatives in the Middle East and beyond.

Chapter 3

The Arabs' Cold War

ISRAELIS CLAIM THAT ARAB STATES ARE SECRETLY SIDING with Israel against Tehran. There is a measure of truth to this, because there is a palpable fear, especially among Gulf Arab states, that Iran's hegemonic ambitions will be strengthened through nuclear blackmail. But the claim of a tacit Israeli-Sunni alliance also partakes of some wishful thinking. However much the Arab regimes loathe the prospect of a nuclear Iran, they also fear the destabilizing passions of their own populations. They know that Iran derives insidious prestige for its rejectionist stance against Israel and much sympathy on the Arab street for what is widely seen as a double standard by which only Israel is allowed to possess nuclear weapons. This delicate political dynamic was revealed in the 2006 Lebanon war, when the "moderate" Arab states at first were surprisingly supportive of Israel's right to defend itself against the predations of the Iranian-backed Hezbollah. Such Arab understanding as there was soon evaporated, however, with the wider popular revulsion at the casualties inflicted on Lebanon's civilians.

Sotto voce, the Arab regimes say that a tacit alliance for the containment of Iran would be much easier to construct and maintain if there was a solution to the plight of the Palestinians. This argument also contains a large measure of truth, but points at the same time to one of the many intractable dilemmas of Middle East politics: for it provides incentive for Iran to do everything possible, through its proxies among Palestinian and Lebanese extremists, to frustrate the peace process. And if the Arabs might be secretly relieved by Israeli air strikes that effectively destroyed Iran's nuclear facilities with limited collateral damage, they are greatly anxious about the specter of wider war.

In trying to understand the wider regional dynamics of a confrontation involving Iran, Israel, and America, there are three kinds of evidence to draw on. First is the history of coalition building in the Middle East. Second is the current posture of Arab states and societies regarding Iran's bid for regional influence if not hegemony. Third is informed speculation about how those states and societies will react to military action, or all-out war, involving Israel, Iran, and the United States.

Coalitions Past

Washington has a 50-year history, with successes and failures, of trying to forge coalitions of Middle Eastern states. Though U.S. missionary activity had been extensive since the start of the nineteenth century, and U.S. naval forces had tangled with Barbary pirates, systematic American involvement in the region came only with World War II, when the supply of oil to sustain allied military operations, and the need to deny that oil to Nazi Germany, became important. This American interest soon led to shared ownership of Saudi energy resources, but America's initial postwar role in the region was otherwise limited. Washington was preoccupied with the stabilization of Western Europe in the face of the Soviet domination of Eastern Europe, pressure on Berlin, and attempts to manipulate Western European politics in favor of communist parties. In Asia, a long U.S. occupation recast Japanese society, Mao's victory swept Washington's allies from China, and war threatened over Korea and Taiwan. In the Western Hemisphere, social revolutionaries were threatening friendly regimes from Cuba to Argentina. From Washington's perspective, Middle Eastern problems could just as well be left for Britain to handle. London had military forces and a substantial base structure in Egypt and the Arabian Peninsula and nearly two hundred years of colonial experience.

British power had been broken, however, by the world wars. Zionist and Arab violence succeeded in ejecting a large British force from Palestine in 1947. Rioting and armed skirmishing challenged Britain's position in Egypt. The decisive, if not final, blow was delivered, ironically, by the United States in 1956, when the Eisenhower administration responded to the British, French, and Israeli invasion of Egypt by demanding the withdrawal of their forces and threatening the United Kingdom with bankruptcy if it failed to comply. Britain's humiliation at the hands of the American ally reinforced the skepticism of impoverished Britons about the sustainability of the imperial project. British prime minister Anthony Eden became known as the last U.K. leader to believe that

Britain was a world power, and the first to demonstrate that it was not.

From Washington's perspective, Britain's declining leverage posed a problem, given Moscow's interest in oil and a warm-water port from which to contest American control of sea lines of communication. America's policy response was the Eisenhower doctrine, a pledge to aid any Middle Eastern state at risk of takeover by communists. This departure followed upon Washington's initial effort to woo the ascendant Gamal Abdel Nasser. In the thinking of the time, secular technocrats, many of whom were found in the armies of the third world, were the key to modernization and, implicitly, Westernization. Nasser and his circle of "free officer" plotters, who overthrew the British dominated monarchy, fit this mold. But Nasser's appeal diminished as his anti-Western and anti-Israeli rhetoric escalated. He had wanted U.S. backing for the Aswan Dam project as well as arms to challenge Israel. His belligerent posture, however, alienated Washington—John Foster Dulles branded him a tin pot Hitler—with the result that the United States withdrew support for the dam. Arms sales were not an option in any case, owing to an agreement among Western powers to limit weapons transfers to the region. The Soviets grasped the opportunity and, through the Czechs, supplied Egypt with a substantial arsenal, while agreeing to finance the construction of the dam at Aswan. With Egypt already lost, the first application of the Eisenhower doctrine was in Lebanon in 1957, when 15,000 Marines landed on the beaches to prop up the conservative, Christian government of Camille Chamoun from a leftist, mostly Muslim challenge.

The Soviets, by coming to Nasser's rescue, managed to leapfrog the CENTO alliance that had been cobbled together by the United Kingdom and United States to contain the southern flank of the Soviet Union. This alliance had constituted the second part of Washington's response to the vexing conjunction of rising Soviet ambitions and waning British power. Known as the Baghdad Pact before Iraq's withdrawal in 1958, CENTO included Turkey, Pakistan, Iran, and the United Kingdom. Though not formally a member, the United States as supplier of arms and money was the de facto linchpin. But the Soviets now had their warm-water port in Egypt, as well as a close relationship with the Egyptian military. Nasser worked against U.S. interests more broadly through the electrifying effect he had on pan-Arab politics. Nasserism, a vague blend of Arab chauvinism, anti-Western bombast, socialist idealism, and rousing optimism paved the way for revolutions in Iraq and Syria and, briefly, to the union of Egypt and Syria. These changes benefited Moscow's geopolitical objectives not only by providing the USSR with ready allies, but also by creating serious problems for the conservative monarchies on which the United States now had to rely. As a matter of necessity, the United States strengthened ties to Saudi Arabia, which, by the mid-1960s was backing a conservative regime in Yemen against 55,000 Egyptian troops fighting on behalf of radical revolutionaries. Jordan also began to receive large amounts of U.S. aid. Iran was allowed to purchase the pick of the U.S. military inventory and, like Jordan, embarked on a long, close relationship with the CIA.

Despite episodic dislocations, America's Middle East alliances proved remarkably durable. Saudi Arabia, with its tremendous energy resources, remained in America's camp despite deep differences occasioned by the Carter administration's arrangement of a separate Egyptian peace with Israel. Egypt ultimately switched sides, jettisoning Soviet advisors in 1972 (to the weird indifference of a complacent White House) and then got help from Washington to secure the return of the Sinai Peninsula from Israeli control. Jordan, perennially vulnerable to the grievances of its majority Palestinian population, Syrian aggression, periodic Egyptian and Iraqi subversion, and its own occasional if formidable blunders, survived as a conservative monarchy in tune with U.S. objectives. The small states on the Arab side of the Persian Gulf made the transition from British to American protection during the Cold War and would likely have supplied the United States with the base access necessary to counter Soviet forces if, as was feared, the Soviets invaded Iran to seize its oil fields. Iran, from the Soviet occupation of Azerbaijan in 1946 until the 1979 revolution, remained a bulwark against Soviet expansion from the north. Turkey joined NATO in 1952. And during the 1980s, Israel provided the United States with military assistance through a series of combined operational contingency plans that would have helped the Sixth Fleet ward off Soviet attempts to control the eastern Mediterranean in the event of war.

There were problems, of course. This period was marked by three major conflicts—the Six-Day War in 1967, the October War of 1973, and the Iran-Iraq War of 1979–1989—and a few relatively minor ones, such as the Israeli siege of Beirut in 1982, with lasting adverse effects. Moreover, the salient U.S. diplomatic achievement during the Cold War, the Camp David Accords—although making future Arab-Israeli wars unlikely—never led to a Palestinian state, let alone the autonomy called for by the Accords; rather, they led to Israel's invasion of Lebanon five years later. We are still dealing with the consequences of this failure today.

It is also true that Washington's success at pitting conservative regimes against radical ones had much to do with dynamics that were independent of U.S. interests and actions. As famously observed by Malcolm Kerr, a president of American University in Beirut killed by Iranian backed militants in 1984, an Arab Cold War prevailed during this period, which dovetailed with the global one. After 1958, Egypt and Iraq contested leadership of the Arab world, each trying to subordinate Syria to its cause. The Saudis along with Jordan were targeted by both radical regimes, whose challenge to the legitimacy of the royal houses appealed to Arabs across the region. The assassination of Jordan's Hashemite king in 1951 and massacre of the Hashemite court in Iraq in 1958 provoked acute anxieties. The United States could offer protection without really cramping Saudi style, which did not allow for accommodation to a Jewish state, nor shrink from use of the oil weapon against America and other friends of Israel in the aftermath of the October War. Likewise, Jordan's entry into the 1967 war against Israel and its backing of Iraq in 1991–1992 did not diminish Washington's friendship. Egypt's conversion from Soviet ally to U.S. client would not have happened had Sadat's domestic standing been sound, which it was not: the cry on the streets of Cairo was "Oh, hero of the [1973 Suez Canal] Crossing, where is our breakfast?" Without the revenue from Sinai oil, Sadat needed the help only a superpower could deliver. But the Soviets were an undesirable and perhaps even dangerous presence: domestic opposition to Sadat's regime came from the left, especially on the campuses. Middle Eastern regimes have never feared invasion as much as subversion.

Thus, Washington's coalition building entailed pushing on the open doors of regimes that badly needed insurance.

The fact remains, however, that as of 1979 the United States had emerged the winner in its regional competition with the Soviet Union. It had unimpeded access to oil, a secure Israeli ally, and well-armed Saudi and Iranian monarchies to defend its interests, all at little cost in American blood and treasure.

After 1979, Washington's bid to fashion another coalition, this time against Iran, worked well enough for the same reasons. Iran's predatory rhetoric in the triumphant year following the overthrow of the Shah provoked an extremely hostile reaction in the region. Accordingly, Iraq's invasion of Iran was eventually supported by the Arab oil-producing states, which kept Baghdad afloat as its revenues and reserves were drained by the war. Tehran ended the war with just one regional ally, Syria, whose Ba'ath party was opposed to Iraq's, and who therefore supported the enemy of its enemy. Again, Washington did not get everything it wanted. Only Oman, for example, granted formal base access. (Access to bases in Kuwait, Bahrain, the UAE, and Qatar was to follow a decade later.) There was a reluctance to be seen as too close to America; exceptions to this rule depended, naturally, on threat perceptions. When Kuwaiti shipping proved vulnerable to Iranian attack in the latter stages of the Iran-Iraq War, Kuwait asked the United States, and the Soviet Union, to reflag its vessels in the hope of discouraging Iranian harassment. Yet a few years before, Kuwait had felt secure enough to refuse Washington's choice of ambassador because he had served as consul general in Jerusalem.

Upon Saddam's invasion of Kuwait, American coalition-building efforts shifted to war against Iraq. Choreographed by President George H. W. Bush and his secretary of state, James A. Baker, the formation of the Gulf War coalition has become an icon of effective diplomacy. It was that, but it was also a largely cost free concession for participants who asked for, and received, substantial rewards for joining. Syrian animosity toward Iraq, which Damascus accused of subversion, was unconfined and its need for Saudi cash so urgent that its deployment of an infantry division to Saudi Arabia, where it saw no combat, was fairly easy to arrange. Similarly, Egypt needed cash transfusions and, as we have seen, resented Iraq's claim to supremacy in the Arab world, especially when Baghdad's self-assertion derided Egypt's failure to humble Israel. The Saudis feared that they were next in line, after Kuwait, and were moved to join the coalition by a well-developed instinct for self-preservation. The achievement of U.S. diplomacy was to marshal a coalition by recognizing and exploiting these conditions and to do so swiftly and seamlessly. Even more impressive was the skillful manipulation of the UN Security Council and Arab League to persuade the Arab street that war against Iraq was a legitimate undertaking, when many Arabs admired Saddam Hussein's toughness and nursed more than just a mild resentment against a grasping and *nouveau riche* Kuwait. The promise of vigorous action to promote a Palestinian-Israeli agreement, which led eventually to the Madrid conference and the Wye Accords, was an important part of the bid to win the acquiescence of Arab publics.

Coalitions Present

The almost mythical status of the first Bush administration's coalition formation in the first Gulf War has made coalition building the inescapable option in the current crisis, even if the balance of costs and benefits is difficult to establish. The coalition that the Obama administration wants to marshal would consist of the same countries that were aligned against Iran in the wake of the Islamic revolution. The "GCC plus 2," as it has been dubbed, includes the six Gulf Cooperation Council members plus Jordan and Egypt.

The logic of America's latest effort was unpacked by the director of national intelligence, Admiral Dennis C. Blair, in congressional testimony in February 2010. In his prepared statement, which cast Iran as the center of an "arc of instability," he observed that

> Iranian leaders perceive that regional developments—including the removal of Saddam and the Taliban, challenges facing the United States in Iraq and Afghanistan, the increased influence of HAMAS and Hizballah, and, until recently, higher oil revenues—have given Tehran more opportunities and freedom to pursue its objective of becoming a regional power. This perception has produced a more assertive Iranian foreign policy in which Tehran has focused on expanding ties in Iraq, Afghanistan, and the Levant to better influence and exploit regional political, economic, and security developments.

He added that "Iran's influence in Iraq, its enduring strategic ties to Syria, pursuit of a nuclear weapons capability, and the success of Tehran's allies—HAMAS and Hizballah—are fueling Iran's aspirations for regional preeminence." Washington, according to Blair, would need to put its thumb on the other side of the scales in the form of "strong tools—from military force to diplomacy in the region and good relationships with the vast majority of states," because "Arab Sunni leaders are struggling to limit Iran's gains; Saudi Arabia's more activist regional diplomacy falls short of significantly constraining Iran's freedom of maneuver."[1]

This is a sober assessment. Iran is indeed active on a number of fronts—although whether this represents a master plan or shrewd opportunism is open to question. In Iraq, where its access is better than anywhere else, Tehran is perpetuating a history of interference. In the 1970s, the Shah's support for independence-minded Iraqi Kurds posed a serious obstacle to Ba'athist control over the country, ultimately forcing Saddam's acceptance of a humiliating settlement over control of the Shatt al-Arab. The meddling continued in the 1980s with support for antiregime Shi'a agitprop. This failed to disrupt Baghdad's war effort or pull at the seams of Iraqi society, but did spur Iraq to provide safe haven for the Mujahideen al-Khalq, a terrorist group that drew clerical blood in Iran. Iran also might have supported the 1991 Shi'a revolt in southern Iraq, although whatever assistance it provided could not impede the Iraqi regime's brutal suppression of the uprising.

America's decapitation of Iraq in 2003, followed by a civil war in which U.S.-backed Shi'a forces routed the dispossessed Sunnis, has left Iran in a strong position to influence Iraqi foreign policy and manipulate domestic politics. How strong remains to be seen. Parties such as the Supreme Iraqi Islamic Council, which was launched by Iran to reciprocate Iraq's creation of the Mujahideen, are on the wane, as others, led by Prime Minister Nuri al-Maliki, consolidate their ascendancy. These political groupings have a strong nationalist orientation that is not really compatible with subordination to an Iranian agenda. Iran publicly opposed a 2008 status of forces and strategic framework agreement that helped legitimate (and regulate) the U.S.-Iraq military relationship; at the end of the day, however, Iran did not break with Maliki over it. Still, it seems likely that Iran will enjoy a privileged relationship with Iraq, even as Baghdad seeks an independent voice and freedom of action. This outcome resulted from a U.S. grand plan, not an Iranian one. Tehran was simply given a strong hand and has played it competently, by providing goods, services, and credit, supporting militias that created problems for the coalition in order to hasten an American departure, and serving as an indispensable mediator to help Iraqis solve contentious issues, like the status of the "Mahdi Army," controlled by America's *bête noire*, Moqtada al-Sadr, in the wake of Maliki's military campaign to humble his Shi'a rivals in February 2008.

In thinking about Iran's influence in Syria, it is important to remember that the two countries have been allies for 30 years, longer than the United States had been an ally of Britain's when it established Lend-Lease in 1941. Their current, close affiliation emerged from decades of mutual support, Iranian investment in Syria, common foreign policy goals vis-à-vis Iraq, Lebanon, and Israel, and shared status as pariahs in the West, a badge that both regimes carry with self-conscious pride. This intimate relationship was born as much of necessity as design. Mutual need and obligation continue to give it momentum. Presumably, their friendship will vary proportionally with the degree of their respective diplomatic isolation, which is unlikely to lessen soon.

Iran's relationship to Hezbollah extends nearly as far back as its link to Syria. Hezbollah was forged in the crucible of heavy fighting between the Israeli army and the Palestine Liberation Organization in the early 1980s. Its leadership was inspired by the piety and anti-colonialism of Ayatollah Khomeini, and its fighters were trained by Iran's Revolutionary Guard Corps. For Iran, Lebanese Hezbollah represented the clerical regime's only possibility, after the hopes of 1979 had been shattered, of birthing a revolutionary Islamic state elsewhere in the Middle East. Tehran's umbilical connection to Hezbollah, which depended on Syrian cooperation, also put Iran on the border with Israel and made it a player in the resistance to Israel's existence; indeed, after the 1973 war, the only one. Sponsorship of Hezbollah also gave Iran the reach to pay back the United States for its support of the hated Shah and commitment to Israeli security. It is true, therefore, that Iran rides the strong horse of Lebanese politics today, but only because it groomed the pony 30 years ago and provided the fodder steadily and generously ever since. The failure of the other confessional groups to mobilize successfully against Hezbollah is, in part, a function of their inferior leadership and organization, but also a result of their inability to challenge Hezbollah's claim to be Lebanon's firewall against Israeli aggression. This assertion might be specious, but it is widely believed. Israel's unilateral withdrawal in 2000 substantiated Hezbollah's boast even as it weakened the Lebanese government's credibility. Hezbollah will always have to rely on an autonomous military capability to retain its veto power over Lebanese government policy. Thus, an Israeli-Palestinian accord, or, for that matter, peace treaty with Syria, would presumably be insufficient to alter Hezbollah's determination to retain its arsenal. It would, however, facilitate international and Lebanese efforts to push Hezbollah toward disarmament—and a normalized status within Lebanese society—along the lines of the successful Anglo-American push for "decommissioning" of the Provisional IRA's weapons in 1998.[2]

Tehran's support for Hamas, in contrast, is relatively recent. It too is the result of a windfall: the collapse of the 2000–2001 peace initiatives, the beleaguerment of the Hamas winners after the 2006 Palestinian Authority elections and the resulting civil war, which left Hamas in control of Gaza. Tehran supplied Hamas with the weaponry whose use triggered Israel's Operation Cast Lead in December 2008. Among the items provided by Iran were 122 mm rockets and heavy mortars, as well as IEDs of the same construction as those used against U.S. forces in Iraq. Resupplies came via Sudan and Egypt; arms were smuggled into Gaza through a dense labyrinth of tunnels. This sort of assistance can enable Hamas to start wars, but not to finish them. That prerogative still belongs to Israel. When it was over, the Gaza war left 1,400 Palestinians dead, urban infrastructure damaged, and intra-Palestinian politics even more strained, as Fatah accused Hamas of fecklessly provoking the disaster and Hamas indicted Fatah for collaboration with the enemy. Iran demonstrated its steadfastness, but only as a willingness to fight to the last Palestinian. Its public posture was notably low-key.

Hamas may be an asset for Tehran, but is hardly a key to Iranian regional hegemony. Palestinian attitudes toward Iranian influence are ambivalent; crowds in Gaza have shouted "Shi'a, Shi'a!" when protesting against Hamas, an expression of contempt for its reliance on Iran.[3] There is evidence that Hamas itself is split over the wisdom of a creeping Iranian alliance.

Elsewhere, Iran seems to have made few inroads. To the extent that the mullahs had any sway over Shi'a opinion in the eastern province of Saudi Arabia, a combination of al-Saud cooptation and coercion has countered it. Bahrain's Shi'a majority still engages in occasional street protests over discrimination by the Sunni minority, but these are quickly dispersed. Shi'a militancy has been effectively suppressed by a security service, run by a

British general until 2000. Here as well, charm offensives by the ruling family help relieve the pressure. In 2009, for example, the king pardoned 178 activists. In Kuwait, the large minority of Shi'a citizens participates politically and seems reconciled to Sunni rule.

Tehran's most recent opportunity to influence events far from Iran lies in Yemen, where the government has been engaged in bloody fighting against Zaydi rebels in the north.[4] The insurgents, named Houthis after their late leader Abd al Malik al Houthi, want a greater share of resources from a regime that has viewed them with suspicion since 1962, when the Zaydi elite was displaced in that part of Yemen by the emergence of the Yemen Arab Republic.[5] Zaydis are Shi'a, although their embrace, centuries ago, of the Hanafi approach to Islamic law places them closer to Sunnis in matters of practice than to the Twelver Shi'a in Iran. Perhaps to internationalize their cause, or just attract Iranian help, the rebels attacked a Saudi border post in 2009, killing a guard. Whether this stratagem drew Iranian assistance is unclear, but it did provide Saudi Arabia with a pretext to characterize the Houthi revolt as yet another Iranian assault on the regional order and to go on the counteroffensive. This development, in turn, was seized on by Iran as evidence that the Houthis were indeed a besieged Shi'a minority community in need of Iranian help. Iran's foreign minister, Manouchehr Mottaki, warned ominously, "Countries of the region must seriously hold back from intervening in Yemen's internal affairs. Those who pour oil on the fire must know that they will not be spared from the smoke that billows."[6] The Yemeni government had already accused Iran of supplying the rebels' weapons by ship, although it offered no evidence. What was not quite explained is why the risky business of foreign arms shipments would be required to sustain the rebels' combat power, given that Yemen is famous for being one of the region's most heavily armed nations, and the Yemeni army itself maintains robust sales of its own inventories to rebels and others with ready cash. Some money, however, does seem to flow from Iran to the rebels.

Tehran is happy enough to be seen as a defender of coreligionists against an oppressive government and Wahhabi aggression. The reality, however, is less than the rhetoric of both sides would suggest. The Iranian regime is not well positioned to pick a fight with Riyadh, given Tehran's domestic difficulties and the possibility of stiffening international economic sanctions. The balance of incentives, resources, and capabilities favors Saudi Arabia, for whom the stakes in Yemen are higher than they are for Iran. Against this background, it is a stretch to equate Iranian involvement in Yemen with a serious challenge to the Arab world.

There is a case to be made, however, that the whole of Iranian influence in the region will exceed the sum of its parts. This argument flows from the thesis, first deployed by Vali Nasr, an academic who went to work in 2009 for the Obama administration, that Shi'a Muslims in the Middle East and South Asia, galvanized by the Shi'a *reconquista* in Iraq and the spectacle of a defiant Iran, were poised to challenge the regional order wherever they existed in large numbers. The Shi'a crescent, as it is called by those who fear this scenario, extends from Pakistan to the Levant and corresponds more or less to the region that Admiral Blair labeled an arc of instability, or, decades ago, Carter's national security advisor Zbigniew Brzezinski called "the arc of crisis."[7] Since there are sizable Shi'a populations in Pakistan, Iraq, Saudi Arabia, Kuwait, Bahrain, Lebanon, and Syria—if Alawites are to be counted as Shi'a—the mobilization of Shi'as by Iran, or by the example of Shi'a supremacy and Sunni subordination in Iraq, could, according to this theory, destabilize nearly every country in the region. The transnational nature of Shi'a clerical networks would contribute to such a surge.

This is not a baseless fear. Since the Arab cold war of the late 1950s, Arab states and Iran have at different times used deterritorialized ideologies such as pan-Arabism, pan-Islamism, or shared ethnicity to delegitimize rival governments and manipulate domestic politics in neighboring states. The notion of a shared Shi'a destiny cannot necessarily be dismissed as somehow less compelling to Shi'a than any of the preceding *isms* were to Arabs, Sunni and Shi'a, more generally.

Arab governments appear to be united in these fears. Saudi King Abdullah framed the problem in religious terms, alleging that Iran was trying to convert Sunnis to Shi'ism.[8] "We are following up this matter and are aware of the Shiite proselytism and what point it has reached....This majority will not abandon its beliefs. At the end of the day it is the decision of the majority of Muslims that counts." He added, reassuringly, "Other creeds do not appear able to infiltrate the Sunni majority or undermine its historical authority." Hostile references to "Shi'afication" (*teshayyu'*) by clerical authorities and politicians in Sunni societies have become rife.[9] The theme was picked up, notably by Jordan, as it was becoming clear that Iraq was destined for Shi'a domination. In Jordan, where there are virtually no indigenous Shi'a, King Abdullah spoke darkly in 2004 of a Shi'a crescent piercing the heart of the Middle East. He later tried to downplay the sectarian tone of his original formulation, implying that use of "Shi'a" had merely been a euphemism for Iran.[10]

Egypt has focused on both the sectarian and state-sponsored Shi'a threat. Police arrested 26 operatives of a 49-member Hezbollah cell in April 2009 that Cairo accused of plotting to blow up Egyptian and Israeli targets in Sinai, attack ships transiting the Suez Canal, and overthrow the Egyptian government. This large multinational cell was accused of doing the larger bidding of Iran, Syria, and Qatar. A special court convicted the 26 in April 2010. Qatar, despite being an informal ally of the United States, has worked diplomatically to advance Hezbollah's interests in Lebanon and, through its activism and control of Al Jazeera, to grab some of Egypt's fading regional authority. Here, too, the issue was less Shi'a self-assertion, despite fevered allegations of proselytization of Egyptian Sunnis, than concern about Iranian maneuvering for strategic advantage. Egyptian foreign minister Ahmed Abul Gheit phrased it grandiloquently: "Iran and Iran's followers want Egypt to become a maid of honor for the crowned Iranian queen when she enters the Middle East."[11] Its chief agent, according to Egypt's state-controlled press, was "the monkey sheikh," Sayyid Hassan Nasrallah, the spiritual leader of Hezbollah.[12] One gets the sense that the religious language used to characterize growing alarm about Iranian ambitions is intended to win public support for anti-Iranian policies that are otherwise unpopular. Shi'ism, in contrast to anticolonial theater and launching of rockets at Israel, is viewed with suspicion and disdain. Whether stoking fears of Shi'afication will seriously undermine admiration for Iran and its Hezbollah client for their belligerent blend of anti-Zionism and anti-Semitism is unclear. Interestingly, the Muslim Brotherhood line, propagated through much of the Sunni Arab world, is that Shi'a-Sunni comity is imperative if the potential of the Middle East is to be unlocked.

In any event, the anxieties unleashed by the prospect of a Shi'a revival have to be balanced against the effectiveness with which these majority Sunni countries have dealt with the threat of subversive ideologies in the past. The conservative monarchies that faced down pan-Arabism and Ba'athism are mostly still in power. The one exception, King Faisal's Iraq, failed to survive because it handled its relationship with Britain, on the one hand, and with Iraqi society, on the other, so oafishly. Egypt and Syria, both of which were tested by violent Islamist uprisings, emerged strengthened from the encounter. Even Iraq's Ba'athist regime, which endured sanctions, Kurdish and Shi'a insurgencies, and costly wars with Iran and the United States, did not crack until it was physically overthrown by an American-led invasion. Since the war, authoritarian regimes not only resisted the pressure of the latest *ism* to confront them—democratization—but also used the excesses of the civil war in Iraq and Washington's rhetoric about a war on terrorism to justify renewed repression.

The question is whether Arab apprehensions about Iran can be transformed into a strategically significant coalition. Israel seems to think so. In December 2009, Israeli deputy foreign minister Danny Ayalon published a letter in the Arabic daily *Al-Sharq al-Awsat* in which he argued, passionately, that the "Iranian regime has many tentacles spread out across the region sowing destruction and despair amongst the people....Iran seeks to hold an entire region, including its own people, to ransom and keep it engaged in conflicts orchestrated and directed from Tehran." Despite what many in the Arab world might think, "The enemy of the people of Lebanon is not Israel, but Hizbullah. The enemy of the Palestinian people is not Israel, but Hamas. The enemy of the Egyptian people is not Israel, but militant Islamist opposition groups. All of these groups," he explained, "and many others, receive their commands from Iran, who wish to control and suppress any aspirations the region has towards freedom and advancement." He concluded as follows:

> For the first time in many years, we find ourselves on the same side in seeking to quell and defeat the forces of extremism and destruction in our region. While many see the threat from Iran directed solely at Israel, we in the region know differently. Together, we understand the menace that emanates from the extremist regime in Tehran. A regime that seeks to export its extremist ideology across the region and beyond, while arming terrorist groups that seek to destabilize moderate Sunni regimes and aiming for hegemonic control of the Middle East and far beyond.[13]

Tellingly, however, Ayalon did not say what these Arab states at risk of subjugation by Iran and its proxies are supposed to do. The only positive steps, he seemed to imply, would be to recognize the concessions Israel has made to the Palestinians, including fewer roadblocks and pledging to halt settlement activity outside of Jerusalem for 10 months. On the basis of these concessions, Ayalon presumably hoped the Arab states could adopt a less critical posture toward the Jewish state. It is not clear how conforming more closely to insidious Iranian typecasting of Sunni state behavior would somehow enable these regimes to win the battle for hearts and minds in the Middle East.

Ayalon's appeal has had echoes in the United States. Walter Isaacson, for example, has proposed the creation of MATO, the "Middle East Anti-Terrorism Organization," which would include Israel once it had cleared things up with the Palestinians. Much of this conceptualizing prompts the thought, "…and if my grandmother had had wheels, she'd have been a car." Although some forms of overt cooperation that are now infeasible would become possible, or even likely, were the two- state solution to be realized, prospects for formal alliances that include Israel are remote. As it is, in areas that relate to security and particularly on counterterrorism, there has been the sort of tacit cooperation envisaged by Isaacson, but on a bilateral basis between Israel, Jordan, and Egypt.

The kind of cooperation that can best contain the spread of Iranian influence was demonstrated by U.S.-Saudi coordination of funding not just for reconstruction of Lebanon after the 2006 war, but covert funding in support of the Siniora government's effort to weather the political and military assault by Hezbollah that began in December 2006 and crescendoed in May 2008. But this sort of collusion does not always obtain, even with respect to Iran. The Saudis provided funding for Sunni groups to destabilize the very Shi'a government in Baghdad that the United States was helping to consolidate, because, from the perspective of the Al-Saud, a Shi'a-controlled Iraq was tantamount to an Iranian tool, and therefore a threat to Saudi interests. Nevertheless, when Washington and Riyadh are aligned, the combination can get results.

It is less obvious, though, what a regional coalition could deliver that its members would not be doing anyway as an autonomic response to Iranian self-aggrandizement. The GCC plus 2 do not sit on the UN Security Council as permanent members and thus cannot influence deliberations on sanctions. Nor, for example, would the Saudis use against the Chinese the oil weapon they wielded in 1973, should Beijing veto a Security Council resolution for stronger sanctions against Iran (although the Obama administration has asked the Saudis to reassure Beijing that they will replace Iranian oil that might be cut off if tensions rise).

The odds that a combination of pressure and diplomacy will produce effective limits on Iran's nuclear program do not look very good, and there is little reason to suppose that they can be much improved through the workings of an informal Arab-Israeli-American coalition. So the real logic of building such a coalition probably has more to do with the need—as yet unutterable—to equip key countries to contain Iranian power once Tehran has attained a nuclear weapons capability. This should be doable. Nuclear weapons are now 65 years old, and there is little or no evidence in that history to suggest that their mere possession offers their possessors any particular coercive powers. The United States coerced Japan to surrender, but only after it had actually used the weapons to destroy two cities. As Harvard's Steven Miller has observed, American possession of thousands of nuclear warheads has never meant that even dependent allies will do Washington's bidding—unless they deem it to be otherwise in their interests. It is not obvious why Iran's possession of a far more rudimentary capability should give it any greater coercive power. Indeed, as Miller further observes, whether one calls the adjacent body of water the "Persian Gulf" or "Arabian Gulf," it is—in the strategic currency of naval power and bases access—an American lake. It is hard to imagine that Iranian progress toward a nuclear weapon capability would inspire Gulf Arab states to renounce American protection.

This does not mean, however, that the new situation would be without risk. There is reason to worry that the limited political utility of nuclear weapons will not be obvious to an Iranian regime that has just expended a huge effort to develop them. In this dangerous transitional period, Tehran might act as though its weapons capability meant a great deal. Miscalculation and conflict could be the result. In this context, Washington will be relying on the coalition to resist the two forms of pressure that a nuclear-emboldened Iran might apply: insisting that U.S. access to Persian Gulf bases be curtailed; and pressuring Saudi Arabia and other oil producers to peg production—and therefore price—levels to Iran's revenue requirements. Although the natural impulse of these countries will be to balance with the United States against such extortion, this impulse would need to be reinforced. One means of reinforcement, let slip by Secretary of State Clinton, but subsequently withdrawn by the Obama administration, was the prospect of a protective U.S. nuclear umbrella over the Gulf allies. The credibility of extended deterrence, as we know from doubts raised in the latter half of the twentieth century about Washington's willingness to trade New York for Hamburg, or Paris, can never be absolute. The vulnerable members of the alliance need tangible signs of their patron's commitment and a modicum of confidence in their own defensive capabilities. Likewise, the patron needs to know that its forces are interoperable with its allies' equipment and infrastructure in the event these become necessary to use, and that its forces have unimpeded access to staging bases.

Hence the similarity of the U.S. approach to shaping the GCC plus 2 coalition to previous efforts at creating strategic partnerships. Arms sales are deemed essential. Only if coalition members are secure can they be expected to run the risks of challenging a powerful regional rival. Accordingly, the Bush and Obama administrations set in motion a $20 billion arms package for Saudi Arabia,

Bahrain, Kuwait, Oman, Qatar, and the UAE configured to improve air defense and naval capabilities. At the same time, U.S. military assistance to Israel grew by 43 percent, for a total of $30 billion over the decade. The increase was due partly to Israeli jitters over Saudi Arabia's acquisition of satellite-guided munitions, which, until recently, had been only in Israel's inventory, and partly to replace equipment lost in the 2006 Hezbollah war.[14] These arms transfers are taking place in the context of a stupendous wave of procurement in the region. Outside of the great powers, the highest global spenders in 2008 were the United Arab Emirates, which signed $9.7 billion in arms deals, including $6.5 billion for an air defense system, and Saudi Arabia, which signed $8.7 billion in weapons agreements.[15] In addition, the United States is providing a substantial array of missile defenses to boost the confidence of coalition members worried about the vulnerability of their cities to Iranian ballistic missiles.[16]

American officials have not been shy about advertising these arrangements. In December 2009, CENTCOM Commander General David Petraeus spoke to a gathering of security officials and analysts—including Arabs, Westerners, and Iranians—organized by the International Institute for Strategic Studies in Bahrain. He highlighted the military modernization programs of U.S. allies in the region, and then boasted, "The Emirates' air force itself could take out the entire Iranian airforce."[17]

World on Fire?

Arrangements intended to buttress the ability of Arab Gulf states to withstand Iranian nuclear intimidation won't reassure a nervous Israel in the near term. Israel may feel compelled, therefore, to take matters into its own hands. The question that then arises will be how these various interests and fears among Arab states will play out at successive stages of the unfolding crisis. For Israel, whether these states acquiesce in an attack they detect while it is underway is undoubtedly a serious concern. The possibility of detection is high. Jordan's King Hussein reported the flight of Israeli attackers to Iraq in 1981 because he saw the aircraft from his perch on the deck of the royal yacht in the Gulf of Aqaba. The Arab states straddling the central and southern routes have acquired very capable air defense systems since 1981; some, as noted, are being upgraded now by the United States. It seems likely that Jordan, Saudi Arabia and Kuwait would be able to detect the overflight of Israeli aircraft. Syria might not see ingressing aircraft, but the ability to blind the Syrians again, after doing so in 2007, is not something Israel can take for granted. If some or all of these governments do spot the air wing that Israel has launched toward Iran, they would have the options of alerting Tehran, attempting to intercept the intruders,[18] or simply remaining silent. In the unlikely event that Israel chose to overfly Iraq in the teeth of Washington's opposition, Baghdad would not have an independent ability to detect or intercept the intruders. The United States, which controls Iraqi airspace and would know immediately that Israel had entered it, would be put in a difficult position, probably best managed by avoiding contact with the attackers. Israel, however, is not going to put Washington in this position, even if planners judge that the mission is untenable by any other route.

For all these countries except Syria, the balance of incentives might well lie on the side of silence. All are in the position of free riders, insofar as none wants to see a nuclear-armed Iran and none believes that it would face crippling retaliation for an attack launched by Israel, especially as they would quickly try to outbid each other in condemning Jerusalem after the strike became public. Any of these governments could enhance its domestic and regional popularity by challenging Israeli aircraft within its borders, but a humbled Iran would be the over-riding interest, especially if intercepting aircraft were likely to be shot to pieces by Israeli fighters, which then proceeded to reach their targets in Iran. Domestic and regional respectability would probably be preserved well enough by diplomatic and media criticism of Israel and the United States. Despite this, these states can scarcely be sanguine about the destabilizing effects of a nuclear Iran, or the instability that might follow an Israeli attack. Collectively, they face a no-win situation. Their natural instinct will be to hedge.

The Saudis might be thinking about this scenario in somewhat less timid terms. A flurry of uncorrobo-rated reporting, which probably devolved to a single source, suggested that Prince Bandar bin Sultan, the Saudi national security advisor and former ambassa-dor to the United States, met with an Israeli official in 2008, allegedly to indicate that Saudi Arabia would turn a blind eye to Israeli aircraft on route to Iran through Saudi airspace. If true, this would mitigate the anxiety of Israeli planners to some small degree. But it is not obvious why the Saudis would take the risk of reassur-ing Israel about a course of action that Riyadh could take in any event, without the risk of an embarrassing disclosure of collusion with Jerusalem. Notwithstand-ing the dubious credibility of these reports, some rank-and-file Saudis do seem favorably disposed to the idea of the United States, and with lesser enthusiasm, Israel, attacking Iran's nuclear facilities. According to a recent poll of 1,000 Saudis in Riyadh, Jeddah, and Dammam, one-third of the respondents supported the idea of a U.S. strike, while one-third opposed "somewhat," and another one-third opposed "strongly." One-quarter of urban Saudis supported the prospect of an Israeli attack "to some extent."[19] It seems reasonable to conclude that the Al Saud, if not their Hashemite neighbor, would have some confidence in their ability to ride out popular emotions in the wake of an attack.

It is conceivable that Iran will be unable to distinguish an Israeli attack from an American one, or simply disinclined to make the distinction. The result might be attacks against U.S. installations in neighboring countries, or against the assets or populations of these countries themselves. The range of targets is wide, and falls into two groups: Kuwait, Qatar, Bahrain, the UAE, Saudi Arabia, and Oman, on the one hand; Iraq and Afghanistan, on the other. They present different kinds of challenges. If Iran organizes attacks against the first group of countries, Washington will probably judge that an armed response is necessary and that, in turn, would require the permission of these countries to use their bases for attacks against Iran. This scenario, a nightmare for most of these countries whose infrastructure is vulnerable and who are seeking to expand investment outside of the energy sector, would leave rulers little choice but to accede to U.S. requests. This would lead ineluctably to an intensified U.S. military presence, as Washington deployed more ships and aircraft to defend countries providing base access, while carrying out offensive operations against Iran's military and ultimately its leadership. This could be an open-ended proposition, whereby tit-for-tat attacks mount in frequency and intensity, as each side moves to dominate the escalatory ladder. Given the size and sophistication of U.S. naval forces, the extensive infrastructure available to them along the Arab side of the Gulf, the head start the United States and its partners have exploited to improve missile defenses, and the steps that some basing countries, like the UAE, are taking to manage the consequences of Iranian retaliatory attacks, it seems likely that Washington and its regional allies will be the side that enjoys escalation dominance.

Iraq and Afghanistan are two neighboring battlefields where Iran could try to retaliate by creating problems for the United States. But here the risk of direct U.S.-Iranian fighting could be somewhat lower than in the GCC scenario, since these attacks would be deniable events in the context of ongoing wars. Iranian IEDs killed American soldiers during the height of the Iraqi civil war, but the United States refrained from retaliation even though the origin of the bombs was well established. Opportunities for Iranian action in Iraq will decline as U.S. forces are drawn down, but diplomats and other Americans will still be exposed to violence. U.S. forces in Afghanistan will be vulnerable for several years at least especially since the areas under coalition control closest to Iran are in Spanish and Italian hands and would present ample opportunity for infiltration.

The conflict also could widen to encompass Lebanon, even before an Israeli attack on Iran, should Israel seize on a Hezbollah cross-border action as an Iranian *casus belli* or simply to keep Hezbollah too busy to retaliate for an Israeli attack on Iran. This would not entail a surgical strike. If it happened, an invasion would involve division-sized formations advancing on a broad front, in concert with air and maritime assault, to disarm Hezbollah and push its fighters back far enough to immunize northern Israel against missile attacks. An offensive of this scope could bring Syrian and Israeli forces into contact, sparking full-scale combat and, from an Israeli perspective, ultimately threatening Bashar al-Assad's control in Damascus. The two sides were already talking in these terms in February 2010, with Israeli defense minister Ehud Barak worrying out loud that without "…an arrangement with Syria, we are liable to enter a belligerent clash with it that could reach the point of an all-out, regional war" and Syria's foreign minister, Walid Muallem, warning that "Israel knows that war will move to the Israeli cities." Israel's outspoken foreign minister Avigdor Lieberman's conversation killing rejoinder was that Israel's "…message must be clear to Assad. In the next war, not only will you lose, you and your family will lose the regime. Neither you will remain in power, nor the Assad family."[20]

The bow wave of refugees and retreating Hezbollah fighters in Lebanon set in motion by an Israeli invasion would imperil the fragile truce that now regulates political behavior in Beirut, and possibly trigger renewed civil war. As already noted, the Muslim Brotherhood, unlike other right wing Islamist movements in the Arab world, advocates a Shi'a-Sunni alliance; it could get a tremendous boost. Sunni radicalism of a different and perhaps more dangerous sort would be mobilized by Iran's efforts to generate Arab sympathy and support in the wake of an Israeli attack. These developments would provoke regime fears of instability, reinforcing repressive instincts that will set back political reform, while feeding dissent. Further mutations of the global terrorist virus are among the plausible consequences.

The aftermath of an Israeli attack could lead to further complications, if the United States is drawn into the fray by Iranian retaliation that kills Americans, or jeopardizes

Washington's interests in the Gulf. Coordinated, sustained strikes of mounting violence by U.S. forces could destabilize Iran as regime leaders go into hiding, their communications are degraded, and instruments of state control weaken. Meanwhile, the economy would sink, cut off from trade by the damage dished out to ports, energy and transportation infrastructures, and by the blockade effect of naval operations in the Gulf. Successful Iranian terrorist attacks, commando operations, or lucky hits with cruise or ballistic missiles against Gulf Arab states would hobble economic recovery on the other side of the Gulf, put upward pressure on oil prices, and lead to an exodus of Westerners still essential to the smooth operations of the GCC littoral states. Terrorist attacks are also likely to be launched by Iranian sympathizers exploiting the cover of a large Iranian expatriate population. A slow or clumsy response to attacks would shake popular confidence in ruling families whose legitimacy depends, even now, on a degree of paternalism. The sharp expansion in the U.S. military presence in the Gulf could itself engender anti-American sentiment, particularly if the United States was seen as responsible for the crisis because of its support for Israel, or the tough approach Washington had brought to the nuclear issue and which is seen as having led to a third American war in the greater Middle East.

To be clear, there are certainly less apocalyptic alternatives to this world-on-fire scenario. Rather than spiraling out of control, events might track the well-worn grooves of recent crises. Arab leaders could release some of the pressure of popular opinion by distancing themselves from Israel, perhaps withdrawing ambassadors (where they exist), giving state-controlled media full reign to excoriate the Jewish state, and supporting strongly worded resolutions in the UN General Assembly, the Arab League, and the Organization of the Islamic Conference. Summit meetings intended to show resolve—and relevance—would be announced. Some governments might offer humanitarian, technical, or financial assistance to Iran, although follow-through would be spotty and slow. Popular ambivalence about Iran might offset, to some degree, anger at an Israel seen to be out of control and anger at Arab regimes and the United States for their failure to contain it. All the parties will have strong incentives to avoid escalation. Whether these will trump emotional or spasmodic responses to a range of potent provocations is hard to predict. The momentum of rhetoric could combine with poor judgment to unleash an escalatory dynamic, as in June 1967. But Arab states are more mature now than they were in the wake of decolonization and more secure than they were in the spring of 1967. Regimes have since demonstrated a convincing ability to manage violent opposition.

Still, an Israeli decision to risk indeterminate war with the Islamic Republic might well lead into uncharted territory. This means more than the unexceptional notion that the use of force often carries unintended consequences. It suggests, rather, that an Israeli attack on Iran would be momentous, transforming the regional order in ways that cannot be inferred from past wars. From this perspective, there is simply no way to think coherently about this future and no way to prepare for it. In 1967, for example, neither Egypt nor Israel could have anticipated the long-term effects of its respective decisions: Egypt's decision to blockade Israel while calling for its annihilation; Israel's decision to preempt an Arab assault by attacking Egypt and Syria, and then turn its guns on an imprudent Jordan. These choices permanently restructured Israeli politics, led to a multigenerational Israeli occupation and an ongoing succession of devastating wars, fueled the rise of Islamist politics, and hastened the decline of Egypt as the preeminent power in the Arab world. On the other hand, the Iranian revolution triggered deep and plausible fears of a fatally weakened regional system, in which the regimes on which Washington relied would be swept away by revolutionary fervor flowing from Tehran. As we now know, these anxieties were not to be actualized. Thus, it is possible that an Israeli attack against Iran could contain the seeds of a less dystopian future than did the 1967 war. But betting on it would be quite a gamble.

Chapter 4

Diplomacy's Struggle

ISRAEL HAS ITS OWN NUCLEAR ARSENAL, CONTAINING, according to various estimates, between 60 and 400 warheads with a triad of delivery vehicles: airplanes, land-based missiles, and submarine-based missiles.[1] This nuclear deterrent has been widely known for decades, but never officially acknowledged. Nor has Israel ever brandished its nuclear weapons for the purpose of bluster or intimidation. Its official posture is one of strict ambiguity; Israel says it will not be the first to "introduce" nuclear weapons to the region, meaning that its nuclear arsenal will be neither tested nor announced. Former prime minister Yitzhak Rabin went further, stating gnomically and perhaps ominously that Israel will not be the first country to introduce nuclear weapons to the Middle East, nor will it be the second. In this regard, though they don't quite fit the bill of a "virtual" nuclear weapons state—since they do have the actual weapons—the Israelis have proven to be pretty good models for how such a state should behave. By not declaring their capability, they relieve some of the political pressure on neighboring states to follow suit. The Israeli nuclear arsenal has not been an overt factor in any of Israel's wars. It is a classic, ultimate deterrent for a people who have known, in living memory, what it means to be the objects of annihilation. Having never signed the Non-proliferation Treaty (NPT), moreover, Israel has not violated it.

Yet the Israeli nuclear arsenal does violate, in the minds of many Arabs, fundamental notions of fairness. A previous chapter emphasized the concept of justice as particularly resonant in the Arab world. Though no doubt fed and reinforced by colonial and postcolonial history, this is hardly a uniquely Arab trait. Iran, of course, appeals to the claims of injustice and double standards favoring Israel. And as with Iran's other appeals, this one rings with varying degrees of resonance at different levels and locations in the Middle East. Saudi and some other Gulf leaders are extremely worried about the Iranian nuclear project—to the point of arguing privately, according to some sources, for U.S. or even Israeli military action. Arab populations, including, to a significant degree, journalists, intellectuals, and other elite opinion makers, complain that Iran is unfairly held to a different standard than Israel, and are unmoved by counter-arguments that the Israelis have not employed their nuclear capabilities for purposes of intimidation. More alarming, they are also receptive to Iran's claims that it alone is ready to stand up to Israel, in contrast to acquiescent Arab states. Again, there is an observable difference between the populations of Gulf Arab states, where a sense of Iranian threat is sharpest, and Arabs of the

Levant, where considerations of prestige and taking sides in the confrontation with Israel are more salient. A 2009 debate in the Egyptian Shura Council, the consultative upper house, featured arguments from several opposition members that Egypt needs a nuclear weapons program to balance Israel's.[2] Lakhdar Brahimi, the former Algerian foreign minister and UN special envoy, has argued that that although Arab governments have submitted to the nuclear double standard against the views of their own populations, sooner or later governments will have to adjust their policies to reflect the strong popular feelings, because the reverse—Arab peoples coming to accept the double standard—is simply not going to happen.[3] This tension is one reason that Egypt and other Arab states, all of whom have adhered to the NPT, have been pushing for decades for a nuclear-weapons-free zone in the Middle East, which would include Israel. Israel maintains that it cannot consider such an idea until such time as it enjoys real peace with all of its neighbors. The Arabs, in turn, argue that the Israeli exception is unsustainable and creates a dangerous dynamic whereby, instead of peace, there could be heightened tensions amidst nuclear proliferation—a dangerous dynamic indeed. Of course, to paraphrase Gibbon, "unsustainable" circumstances can be sustained for quite some time.

The perceived unfairness of Israel's nuclear status may have strained regional forbearance, but it is Iran's nuclear program that threatens to break it. As the Iranian nuclear crisis has worsened, there has been a striking and rather sudden interest in nuclear power throughout the Middle East. There are legitimate energy, economic, and environmental reasons for much of this nuclear renaissance, and there are specific domestic drivers in countries such as Egypt, where Gamal Mubarak, son of the president, has taken up the nuclear-energy project as a worthy symbol of techno-nationalist prestige, which he hopes will help him in his campaign to succeed his father.[4] At least one state, moreover, the United Arab Emirates, has signed a technology agreement with the United States in which it abjures its own uranium enrichment and accepts other safeguards; the agreement constitutes the gold standard for making a nuclear energy program as proliferation-proof as possible.[5]

There is little doubt, however, that some of the renewed interest in nuclear power is driven also by hedging strategies. Arab states, and possibly Turkey, want to develop the human capital and technical infrastructure for nuclear technology that would bring them closer to a weapons capability for the day they decide they want or need it. The further development of these dual-use technologies appears unstoppable, given the resurgent global interest in nuclear energy motivated by energy and climate-change worries.

This dynamic brings the Middle East closer to the proliferation cascade that gives many strategic experts sleepless nights. Tipping points might include a final, obvious failure of diplomatic efforts to restrain Iran's nuclear drive; Iranian threats against its neighbors, or actual military conflict involving Iran and Gulf Arab states; an exhaustion of patience with the double standards built into the nonproliferation regime; a collapse of confidence in American strategic skill or commitment to the region; or an Israeli decision to abandon its doctrine of nuclear ambiguity, perhaps because it felt the need to make its deterrent capabilities against Iranian nuclear attack clear and therefore more credible. An Israeli preemptive attack against Iranian nuclear facilities that intensified Iran's determination to build nuclear weapons and leave the NPT could be another tipping point.

These are potential dangers, not predictions. There are forms of strategic reassurance the United States could offer, the most plausible being a set of security guarantees, to prevent a proliferation cascade. The model for such reassurance was the American nuclear guarantee to Cold War allies in Europe as well as Japan. Circumstances are different, of course; the intimacy of the European alliance is unlikely to develop between the United States and Saudi Arabia. Still, it is worth remembering that in early years of the Cold War, there were considerable fears of West Germany going nuclear. These fears seem almost absurd today. Skillful diplomacy and strategic determination can prevent worst-case outcomes.

Nonetheless, a big part of the concern about Iran's nuclear ambitions derives from the grim intuition that the NPT is under severe strain. North Korea has conducted a second nuclear test. India and Pakistan have been nuclear weapons states for more than a decade now without suffering any grave consequences (unless you count their near-nuclear war in the summer of 2002 as a grave consequence). Many sensible observers fear that if Iran goes nuclear, an ensuing proliferation cascade in the Middle East would reduce the NPT to a joke. There is little confidence that a world of 15 or 20 nuclear powers can be managed without a real nuclear war breaking out.

The original NPT was based on a grand bargain under which the recognized nuclear weapons states promised to work toward eventual dismantlement of their own arsenals. Without this promise, the idea that the rest of the world would allow just five countries to enjoy a permanent nuclear monopoly never made much sense. During the Cold War, the promise could be filed under business for the distant future. But the Cold War ended 20 years ago.

The Nuclear World

Some two months into his presidency, President Obama told an audience in Prague that the United States had not forgotten its promise, and would work with other nuclear powers on steps to meet it.[6] Insisting that he was "not naive," and acknowledging that the destination might not be reached in his lifetime, the president nonetheless committed the United States to the goal of a world without nuclear weapons. This is a radical vision, even if it was already implied in the NPT, and faces reasonable opposition from many who argue that nuclear weapons cannot be uninvented. Because the knowledge for building them, say the skeptics, will always be available to dangerous and evil regimes, it will always be incumbent upon status quo powers to maintain at least limited nuclear arsenals for the purposes of deterrence.

Before Obama, the only U.S. president to embrace seriously the goal of total nuclear disarmament was Ronald Reagan, who discussed the idea in summit meetings with Mikhail Gorbachev. Reagan's enthusiasm for this vision was considered, at best, another indication that he was a man of clear and straightforward moral convictions without too much concern for the details or, at worst, as evidence that he was dangerously detached from global strategic reality. Some of Reagan's advisers were openly embarrassed by his antinuclear sentiments.[7]

Yet in January 2007, four elder statesmen—Reagan's secretary of state, George Schultz; Henry Kissinger, who held the same job under Nixon and Gerald Ford; William Perry, secretary of defense under Bill Clinton; and former senator Sam Nunn—published a *Wall Street Journal* op-ed arguing that it was time to adopt and start serious steps toward implementing Reagan's vision of a nuclear-free world.[8] On one level their campaign is another example of the observable phenomenon that old age often radicalizes; this can happen especially to former men of power who, upon retirement, have cause to ponder the implications of their previous actions. On another level, their campaign reflects the conclusion that although mankind thinks it has gotten used to nuclear weapons, it has not tamed them; their continued existence and abundance make it mathematically probable that one day they again will be used, with horrifying consequences.

The four elder statesmen, and now the president of the United States, were also taking clear sides in a somewhat obscure philosophical argument about the causes and nature of nuclear proliferation. There is a strong school of thought, part classical realist and part hawk-neoconservative, which holds that a state's decision to acquire nuclear weapons is not subject to international treaty obligations, global "norms," or sentimentally derived moral considerations. By endorsing the opposite side of this argument, Kissinger, Nunn, Perry, Schultz, and Obama were embracing what can be described as a "European" view of the importance of multilateral cooperation and the power of example exercised by great powers and established nuclear states.[9]

There is a disconnect, however, between such abstract and even visionary terms at the same time that real events on the ground are blotting out the vision. North Korea and Iran present stark problems for those who dream of unwinding the nuclear clock. Pyongyang has more than earned the overused and otherwise unhelpful label of "rogue" state. It has starved its people, engaged in terrorism against its neighbors, fired missiles over Japan, renounced its membership in the NPT and tested two nuclear devices. Both the Clinton and Bush administrations probably would have been ready to remove its nuclear threat by military means, but Pyongyang has a potent nonnuclear deterrent: more than 10,000 artillery tubes, 500 of which are in range to flatten Seoul.

The Iranian threat is perhaps more insidious. Although it has muddied the waters a bit by violating NPT safeguards obligations, Tehran has nonetheless been writing the book on how to achieve a near-nuclear weapons status within the broad parameters of the treaty. Iran would not be the only country with this "break-out" capability; Japan, it is estimated, could build nuclear weapons in a matter of months if it chose to do so. But Japan, totally transparent, has never given any reason to doubt its nonproliferation commitments. Here, moreover, regime type matters: Japan has not used terrorism as a central tool of state policy, or loudly denied the right of another country to exist.

The extent of Iran's nuclear efforts became evident at more or less the same time as major powers in the UN Security Council were arguing over what to do about Iraq. Over the course of late 2002 and early 2003, that argument turned into a diplomatic train wreck that was, in turn, the fitting opening act to America's ill-prepared invasion. It was against this background that the European states, led by France, Britain, and Germany, resolved to do a better job on the problem of Iran. They wanted to prove that tough diplomacy would work better than a reckless unilateral war. Years of negotiations between the "EU-3" and Tehran followed; the Bush administration, philosophically opposed to diplomatic engagement with "rogue states," but also preoccupied by a deteriorating situation in Iraq, slowly and somewhat grudgingly came to support the European approach. Iran showed enough interest in the talks to suspend its uranium enrichment activities for a spell, but insisted that control of the "fuel cycle" was a "sovereign right," and that permanent or even long-term suspension was not on the table. After Iran returned to building and spinning centrifuges, Russia and China joined the Americans and Europeans to pass a series of surprisingly tough UN Security Council resolutions that mandated suspension of these activities under Chapter VII of the UN Charter, which meant that Iran's actions were considered a "threat to international peace and security." The Security Council's unity on this matter was no small accomplishment, because it established that Iran was in violation of an unequivocal international norm, but it had failed in the main goal, which is preventing Iran from moving closer to a nuclear weapons capability. Though some sanctions have been imposed, Russia and China refused to go along with real game-changing penalties that might have administered an adequate shock to the Iranian system. In any event, it was far from certain that even such harsher penalties would work.

A Theory of Diplomacy

The Europeans had not yet proven, therefore, that "effective multilateralism"—the Brussels slogan for their preferred approach—could be made to work. The Bush administration, on the other hand, seemed unable to internalize the very concept of diplomacy, at least when it came to the Iranian file. "We don't speak to evil" was the line attributed to Vice President Cheney in his successful campaign to convince the administration to ignore the Tehran's demarche of May 2003.[10] In its second term the administration in fact allowed the Europeans to put some impressive offers on the table in America's name, including U.S. technical help to Iran for a peaceful nuclear program shorn of enrichment. Iran by this time may have had grounds for doubting whether the United States would, or even could, deliver on the offer.

The Bush administration's constricted concept of diplomacy extended to a country whose help it really needed if there was to be a peaceful solution to this crisis. That country was Russia. U.S.-Russian relations had deteriorated badly since the moment, in 2001, when Bush met the new president, Vladimir Putin, in Slovenia, and claimed to have seen, through Putin's eyes, into a compatible soul. Much of the corrosion was certainly Moscow's fault; Russia under Putin turned increasingly authoritarian. But it was also the case that the United States since the Clinton administration was unready to concede that Moscow was entitled to much more than marginal influence over the shape of post–Cold War security arrangements in Europe. Russian resentment and even fury about this attitude was palpable.

Each side's views were defensible. From Washington's perspective, the enlargement of NATO to bring in former members of the Warsaw Pact was a way to anchor their new democracies, and posed no threat to Russia unless the Russian concept of its own security required hegemony over its neighbors. From Moscow's perspective, enlargement violated an implicit agreement that that neither side would take unilateral advantage of the end of the cold war. It was not absurd to argue that the movement toward Russian borders of an alliance that had been founded against the Soviet Union constituted the taking of unilateral advantage. Russia was probably ready to swallow the first round of NATO enlargement to countries of central Europe. But the ideology of NATO expansion, that every country has a sovereign right to choose its own alliance, rendered the expansion theoretically unlimited. Russian resentment turned to fury and deep anxiety when NATO declared that the former Soviet Republics of Ukraine and Georgia would one day be members.[11] Both contained unhappy, pro-Russian minorities; in the case of Georgia, small breakaway "republics" had emerged from post-Soviet conflict. When the Georgian president decided in August 2008 to use force to bring one of them back under Georgian control, he found himself in a shooting war with Russia.

Similar contention plagued the American plans for missile defense. Ambitious ballistic missile defenses are a Republican enthusiasm going back to Reagan; Democrats have tended toward skepticism, but Clinton kept the research program alive. Although testing has not been resoundingly successful, the Bush administration decided to lock in the program with actual deployments. In addition to sites in California and Alaska, these were to include 10 silo-based missile interceptors in Poland, and an omni-directional X-band tracking-radar base in the Czech Republic. The Poles and Czechs were initially diffident about accepting installations that they knew would draw Russian ire. Warsaw and Prague came around, however, after the Bush administration offered various tokens of reassurance, including Patriot antiaircraft batteries, an American security agreement (theoretically redundant on top of the North Atlantic Treaty's Article 5), along with special emphasis on the fact that with missile defense facilities would come U.S. military personnel to man them. The packages helped emphasize what NATO had long been trying to deemphasize: that a residual NATO purpose was to protect against the possibility of Russian intimidation and revanchism. Warsaw and Prague found this reemphasis gratifying.

Moscow, by the same token, found it maddening. It tended to contradict the American insistence that Poland- and Czech-based missile defenses were directed not against the current Russian ICBM threat, but against a future Iranian one. The American claim was pretty obviously true, but also beside the point as far as Moscow was concerned. To understand why, it is important to remember that although U.S.-Russian political relations have been completely transformed since the Cold War, their *strategic* relationship is still one of nuclear deterrence based on mutual assured destruction.[12] Hence neither side can be indifferent to developments that affect the strategic balance. It is logical reality that an effective missile shield that expanded beyond the 30 interceptors in California and Alaska and the 10 interceptors that were planned for Poland—and Washington never promised any definite limits on future expansion—would constitute such a development. More precisely, it might give Washington the theoretical capability to launch a first-strike attack against Russian nuclear forces, and then protect the U.S. homeland against Moscow's degraded retaliatory force by intercepting the remaining missiles. In political terms, this scenario is absurd: the United States is not going to launch a nuclear war against Russia. In strategic terms, it is plausible, and indeed no more outlandish than the concept of a nuclear "window of vulnerability" favoring the Soviets that agitated the U.S. strategic community in the 1980s.

So upon assuming power in 2009, the Obama administration inherited what looked like a perverse policy mix. An unproved missile defense shield against a not-yet-existing Iranian long-range missile threat was helping to ruin relations with a key permanent member of the UN Security Council whose help was needed against the much more immediate threat: Iranian nuclear capabilities that are further destabilizing the Middle East. Obama understood that he had to set priorities and make choices. His administration made clear from the start that it wanted a major "reset" of relations with Russia. Political appointees and career diplomats alike indicated that they had high expectations for the help Moscow could offer for increasing diplomatic and economic pressure on Tehran.[13]

In September 2009, Washington announced that it was scrapping the plans for missile-defense facilities in Poland and the Czech Republic, in favor of a mobile defense system, on Aegis destroyers and land platforms, to be deployed much closer to potential Iranian missile-launch sites. The president was immediately accused of preemptively appeasing Russia—betraying the Czechs and Poles in the face of Russian blackmail. This accusation required "a caricature of circular causality," as Mark Fitzpatrick has written: "the plan had to go ahead, all the more so because of Moscow's fierce opposition."[14] The hollowness of the appeasement charge is underscored by the fact that—from a technical-military standpoint—the administration's chosen system is more mature and reliable technology against the short- and medium-range missiles that Iran will be able to field soonest.

Behind the decision was a theory that diplomacy necessarily involves trade-offs and concessions. It is true that Washington won no specific concessions from Moscow in exchange for abandoning the Bush missile defense configuration. Given the technical virtues of the decision, administration officials argued that it was not, in the first instance, about Russia anyway. "We put forward a better plan, a more relevant [solution] to the real problem," said one official. "If it happens to create better cooperation from Russia, good."[15] If there was a more constructive Russian attitude toward the Iran problem, however, the change was subtle. The new Russian president, Dmitry Medvedev, said tougher sanctions would be problematic, but conceded they might be "inevitable."[16] Putin, now in the position of prime minister and deemed to be wielding considerable if not unaltered power, was less forthcoming than that. One can speculate that in the context of troubled relations between Russia and the United States, an Iranian nuclear challenge that is so vexing for American goals and influence in the Middle East is not seen, from Moscow, as all bad. Yet, however ambivalent Moscow might be about joining Washington, Paris, London, and Berlin in an escalating confrontation with Tehran, the Russians often have been moved along by their evident exasperation at Tehran's repeated acts of bad faith.[17]

After Britain, France, the United States, and Russia, the fifth veto-wielding member of the Security Council is China. Britain and France were both fully committed to a harder line, while the Russian question was whether the Western powers and Moscow could reach an interests-based accommodation despite their palpable differences. China, by contrast, was more opaque in its strategic outlook, and arguably more plastic. Emerging as a greater world power, it could be seen to be grappling with how to exercise that power and in what role. On proliferation, it had a separate set of concerns involving North Korea and Japan. These would influence how it viewed the Iranian problem without necessarily being dispositive. Likewise, China's energy interests in the Middle East played a great role, but, as discussed below, these can operate in conflicting directions. Thus, the Iranian problem is partly an unfilled canvass on which Beijing would seek to draw the world in which it expects and wishes to live.

Since the confrontation over Iran's nuclear ambitions started in 2002 and 2003, China has maintained its opposition to proliferation, but has also emphasized the need for diplomacy and recognition of Iran's "national rights." Its idea of diplomacy does not appear to include economic pressures or other moves that might sharpen the confrontation. During the Bush administration Beijing was clearly worried that Security Council resolutions might become a prelude and justification for U.S. military action, as they were in the case of Iraq. Although China voted for all UN Security Council sanctions against Iran up until the time this book went to press, it also joined Russia in keeping them watered down. Meanwhile, Chinese companies have undercut the impact of sanctions on Iran by moving to fill the market niche left by Western firms that have curtailed business and financial dealings. China's policies are also strongly influenced by its voracious energy needs and worries about energy security. These have encouraged Beijing to sign substantial commercial and energy interests in Iran, such as the $70 billion deal in 2004 to develop the Yadavaran oil field. There is some tension, however, between China's policy toward the Iranian nuclear problem and the concerns of those Gulf Arab states upon which China is also greatly dependent for oil. The Obama administration has tried to exploit this tension by encouraging the Saudis to promise to make up any shortfall in oil shipments to China in the event that Iran retaliated against UN sanctions with a supply cutoff.[18] On balance, China may view an Iranian nuclear capability as unavoidable, and perhaps not as unwelcome as the prospect is viewed in the West.

A Theory of Iran

Between 2006 and 2008, the UN Security Council approved five resolutions condemning Iran's nuclear noncompliance and imposing an array of sanctions. These were not terribly painful for the Iranians, but they were complemented by unilateral European and U.S. sanctions, including a quiet campaign by the U.S. Treasury Department that had succeeded in cutting off much or most European banking activities in the country—a real hardship for Iranian companies engaged in international trade. Washington's plan in early 2010, following the failure of renewed negotiations with Tehran, was to move to genuinely "crippling" sanctions such as a ban on the export to Iran of refined oil products—possibly a serious blow to a country that subsidizes low gasoline prices but lacks the refinery capacity to produce more than 60–70% of the gasoline it consumes.

But aside from doubts about the chances of organizing such sanctions, there were renewed concerns in the U.S. administration about measures that would so directly punish the Iranian people. The Green Movement, it was feared, would find it impossible to broaden its popular support if associated with outside powers that were inflicting such hardship on the general population. This concern led to new American efforts to formulate tougher but "targeted" sanctions, especially against companies controlled by the Islamic Revolutionary Guards Corps, which appeared to be consolidating its leading role in the Iranian power structure.

All of this is easier said than done. The goal of more serious sanctions may or may not be reachable, but sanctions themselves are of utterly unproven efficacy. There is a large body of literature about this with very limited conclusions. Cuba stands out as an example of a country that has been subjected to a U.S. embargo for longer than most Americans have been alive, without any obvious results beyond adding to the general impoverishment. Apartheid South Africa and Libya under Gadhafi are countries whose policies were significantly affected by sanctions regimes, but special circumstances were involved for each of them. In the case of South Africa, the English-speaking business community was damaged by the sanctions and was able to exert influence toward ending apartheid through a system that was, for whites, democratic. The Libyan choice of secret negotiations to end the sanctions regime was made by one dictator; Iran, by contrast, however repressive the regime, does not concentrate power and authority in a single figure. There is, to be sure, one important similarity: Iran, like Libya under sanctions, is suffering significantly under an embargo on Western investment in its all-important energy sector. But the most important lesson from the South Africa and Libya cases concerns the time frame; sanctions were in place for 32 years against South Africa and 22 against Libya. Iran's nuclear clock is ticking much faster than that.

Obama's theory of Iran pivoted on a concept of Iran as a normal state. As such, Iran could be moved to compromise on its objectionable policies through carefully structured incentives. It was a reasonable theory insofar as it was a set of principles derived from observed phenomena—Iran's pattern of cautious and pragmatic behavior and its demonstrated willingness to sell out specific groups of Islamists for *raisons d'état* (including Azeris, Uighurs, and Chechens)—but only a theory because it had actually never been tested. In the United States, no White House inclined to follow this course could do so without recourse to Congress because meaningful steps required changes to existing legislation. And Congress was not going to cooperate. Hence the Clinton administration's reliance on executive orders to signal a desire for rapprochement. The problem was that the concessions that could be deployed using these instruments were trivial: permitting import of Iran pistachios, or carpets. The initial test of Obama's theory was the reaction of Iran's leadership to his campaign rhetoric, which abandoned the confrontational impulse of the preceding administration, and to his conciliatory and respectful *Nowruz* (New Year's) message distributed in a diverse array of media. Although the White House did not expect to be rewarded by a warm embrace, it did believe that the *Nowruz* message would give an Iranian regime interested in exploring rapprochement of some sort enough leeway to begin. This is not the way things unfolded, however. Khamenei's reply was indicative:

> Even in this congratulatory message, the Iranian people are accused of terrorism and pursuing nuclear weapons; is this a congratulatory note or the continuation of old accusations?... Really, if anything other than a small part of your language has changed, show it. Has your enmity with the Iranian people ended? Have you released Iran's assets? Have you lifted the sanctions? Have you abandoned propaganda and psychological warfare? Have you ended unconditional support for the Zionist regime?[19]

If Shahram Chubin, one of the West's more astute and informed Iranologists, is right, and what Obama was offering was a way into the new global order, then Obama's signaling was likely to be dismissed by Tehran because the revolutionary *nezam* rejected the very legitimacy of this order. In any case, the failure to reciprocate Obama's gesture of respect undercut Obama's theory of Iran and had the predictable effect of reducing whatever flexibility U.S. domestic politics allowed. Despite the evanescent hope projected by the 2009 Geneva deal discussed below, the regime was never unambiguously or consistently receptive to the new administration's conspicuously earnest overtures. Once the postelection crisis was upon the leadership, Tehran was probably too preoccupied even to notice Obama's restraint. That was the second real test of his theory of Iran. If Iran's leaders were normal, in the sense presupposed by the theory, then they would have seized the opportunity provided by the president's reserved posture toward the mayhem in their country's streets by reverting to the Geneva agreement or through some other concession that would secure their international credibility and undermine the opposition. This was not how things unfolded, either. Despite this outcome, Obama's theory of Iran had been plausible enough and tested by the White House prudently, carefully and inexpensively. The administration, however, is now faced with task of articulating and testing a new theory amid political turmoil in Iran and bitter controversy in the United States.

In thinking this through, the president has had to grapple with the question of whether a nuclear deal with Iran is worth the potential, unpredictable cost of buttressing a repressive regime. When Hillary Clinton traveled to the region in February 2010, she gave a speech in which she observed that Iran's regime was turning into a military dictatorship. The point was that the leadership was somehow even worse than one that was revolutionary and Islamic. Predictably, this assertion generated some eyeball-rolling in the audience, from whose perspective the United States is the backer-in-chief for what they consider to be dictatorships where the military rules behind the scenes, the main example being Egypt.[20] U.S. negotiations with the regime at the presumed expense of the opposition would surely reinforce the skepticism the Secretary Clinton encountered in Doha. It would also be controversial in America, where there were rising calls to reorient U.S. policy toward more overt support for the opposition.[21] Given that progress on the key issue—nuclear enrichment—is likely to be nil, the opportunity cost of going down this path is low. The prospects for achieving U.S. objectives through spontaneous regime change, however, also appeared to be uncertain at best, since the opposition lacks a charismatic leader, is fissiparous, and, for the most part, shares the regime's Islamist agenda and nationalist foreign policy goals.

The dilemma became obvious in the fall of 2009, when Iran and the major powers seemed to be on the verge of a breakthrough agreement. The seeming good news—illusory as it turned out to be—had followed a heightening of tensions as another bit of nuclear cheating was uncovered.

On September 25 President Obama called a press conference on the fringes of a UN meeting he was hosting in Pittsburgh on nuclear disarmament. Flanked by French president Nicolas Sarkozy and Russian president Dmitry Medvedev, Obama announced the discovery of another, hitherto secret enrichment facility near the holy city of Qom. This followed the leaking of a document indicating that the Safeguards Department of the International Atomic Energy Agency (IAEA) believed that Iran had the ability to make a nuclear bomb, and was working on developing a missile system that could carry a nuclear warhead.

Just a few days later, however, there came some much more hopeful news. Following secret negotiations between the United States with other major powers and Iran—with the IAEA acting as intermediary—a deal was announced in Geneva and elaborated upon in Vienna whereby Iran agreed in principle to export the bulk of its stockpile of low-enriched uranium (LEU) to Russia for further enrichment to just under 20 percent, after which it would be sent to France for fabrication into fuel assemblies for the Tehran Research Reactor to produce medical isotopes.

This complex deal was the brainchild of President Obama's top nuclear advisor, Gary Samore, who had learned from the IAEA that Iran was having trouble producing isotopes for its medical needs. The idea was to help Iran with this problem and test its nuclear intentions at the same time through an arrangement would take most of its known stockpile out of the country, at least for a time. To be sure, under the best-case scenario, this draft deal might have provided only a partial technical fix to a huge strategic problem. Shipping most of its LEU out of the country for conversion in this manner would delay by about a year Iran's ability to produce a nuclear weapon, assuming that there were no hidden stocks or functioning clandestine enrichment facilities. That is how long it would take Iran to replace 1,200 kg of the material at its known facility. In theory, the 19.75 percent enriched fuel that Iran would receive in return could contribute to a weapons stockpile if reconverted to gasified form and further enriched. However, it would probably come back to Iran in a form that would make this impractical and obvious if the Iranians tried it: tantamount to a declaration of weapons intent that could well provoke preemptive military action.

The deal soon died. Even at the outset, some experts suspected that Tehran was simply dangling the idea as a delaying tactic while it continued to enrich and move closer to a weapons capability. Subsequently, the proposal became entangled in Iran's ongoing political turmoil. To the dismay of some of their Western well-wishers, key opposition leaders attacked the agreement as a sellout of Iran's sovereign rights.[22] These criticisms may have been motivated by political gamesmanship, or by the opposition's need to burnish its nationalist credentials. The effect, in either event, was much the same: the government pulled back from its earlier commitment.

Even if some such deal were ever to be signed and implemented, though, and put off the prospect of war, or of Iran emerging as a nuclear weapons state, it would also crystallize some hard new realities. The deal would imply acceptance of what the Western powers have repeatedly declared to be unacceptable: Iranian enrichment activities that could put it in a position of permanent near-readiness to become a weapons state. Iran, in a certain sense, would still be a kind of "virtual" nuclear weapons state, in a more recessed condition of virtuality. In effect, a thicker redline would be established, giving the international community an extra year to do something about it, but that "something" could very well mean an escalation leading to war. This new baseline might be established as a more or less permanent situation, with two implications for Middle Eastern and international security.

First, such an arrangement would have unpredictable effects on the political situation in Iran itself. The timing of the announced agreement looked like it was intended, on Tehran's part, to give needed prestige to the regime and thereby demoralize the opposition. Ahmadinejad became the deal's only supporter in Tehran, which suggested he thought he had something to gain from it. The opposition's negative reaction lent credence to this interpretation.

Second, the confrontation with Israel would evolve in a direction that depended, in part, on whether Israel's body politic and its strategic elites could live with the permanent condition of nuclear insecurity that would be contained in such a dispensation. Israeli leaders had long maintained that the nuclear know-how to master uranium enrichment constituted an intolerable "point of no return" on the way to Iran developing a weapons capability. But that redline has already been crossed. Israel still demands the dismantlement of Iran's enrichment program, something that would not have happened under the likely negotiated arrangements that might have followed on from the Vienna and Geneva discussions. The question then is whether sufficient conditions of stability, transparency, and reassurance could be created such that Israel might reconcile itself to such Iranian capabilities. If not, the possibility of Israeli preemptive strikes remains very much on the table.

For years a large contingent of well-informed experts have argued that Iran will never give up enrichment facilities that it has already built, and so the only realistic negotiated solution is one that concedes Iran's right to enrich uranium on its own soil. Among the most prominent of these experts is Thomas Pickering, a retired career diplomat and former U.S. ambassador to the UN, who coauthored a proposal for an international consortium to manufacture nuclear fuel in Iran. There have been variations of the proposal; what they all share is the conviction that it is better to have maximum IAEA oversight of Iran's program rather than the current illegal, but essentially unconstrained, effort. Harvard's Steven

Miller, who supports some such scheme, calls it "managed acquiescence"; he concedes it is not very attractive, but argues it is preferable to any remotely realistic alternative. The IISS's Mark Fitzpatrick, a former U.S. deputy assistant secretary of state for nonproliferation issues, expressed the logic of this position, without fully endorsing it, when he wrote "...on the assumption that Iran will not agree to walk back the programme, but may agree to freeze it, any deal that could be struck today is probably better than the deal that might be possible next year and worse than a deal that could have been possible a year ago."[23] Fitzpatrick is nonetheless skeptical of such proposals because he believes the preponderance of evidence is that Iran really does seek a breakout capability. If so, it is reasonable to ask what a strategy of managed acquiescence would achieve.

The modest answer is that it might be a better way of buying time, with fewer adverse consequences, than military action. With that time, much could happen, including political developments in Iran that would make the prospect of nuclear capabilities less frightening.

It seems clear that the Obama administration would take such a deal if it could get it; Washington's support for the fuel-swap arrangement was evidence of this, even if the official position remained a demand for zero enrichment. In our view, the administration would be right to negotiate an arrangement for managed acquiescence. The only serious opposition to it might come from Israel, and perhaps France, which has taken among the most consistently hard lines against conceding any legitimacy to Iran's program. President Sarkozy took an oblique swing at Obama when he complained, at the September 2009 UN General Assembly, that "we live in a real world not a virtual world. And the real world expects us to take decisions....President Obama dreams of a world with-out weapons...but right in front of us two countries are doing the exact opposite."[24] What Paris does not have, however, is a convincing plan to prevent Iran from going nuclear. It suggests that it might be better to punish Iran with isolation even if this cannot prevent weaponization. "I don't believe in technical fixes to political problems," said Martin Briens, head of the nonproliferation depart-ment of the French Foreign Ministry in February 2010. "Politically," Briens continued, imposing "huge costs" on Iranian defiance would be useful for maintaining the credibility of the non-proliferation regime, even if the defiance, and nuclear program, continues.[25]

After the fuel-swap agreement broke down, President Ahmadinejad released a new volley of bluster: because the United States and other major powers had again proven themselves unwilling to help with Iran's legitimate need for medical isotopes, Iran would now produce nearly 20 percent enriched uranium on its own.[26] This would put it just a technical stone's throw from higher-level, weap-ons-grade uranium. Some French strategists speculated that in the Geneva and Vienna negotiations, the United States and its partners had been suckered into legitimiz-ing this further step on the way to a weapon. Neither the French and other Europeans nor the Obama administra-tion were particularly enticed, therefore, when the pres-idents of Turkey, Brazil and Iran on May 7 announced agreement on a new version of the fuel-swap proposal. Although some well-respected analysts, including Pick-ering, argued that the new proposal should be embraced as basis for further negotiations, the United States and Europeans were more inclined to view it as a Groundhog Day attempt to weaken UN Security Council resolve for further sanctions. Among other problems, the removal of

1,200kg of LEU would now take away less than half of Iran's stockpile, since the centrifuges kept spinning.

The only good news was that Iran appeared to be experiencing technical difficulties with enrichment, making an NPT breakout scenario less plausible in the short term.[27] Otherwise, the situation was very worrying.

Chapter 5

Obama's Words

"We remain a young nation, but in the words of Scripture, the time has come to set aside childish things."

—Barack Obama, January 20, 2009

DURING THE 2008 ELECTION CAMPAIGN, SENATORS Hillary Clinton and John McCain both argued that Barack Obama's remarkable eloquence could not compensate for his manifest inexperience. Clinton's put-downs were the most memorable, as at a rally in Rhode Island where she mocked Obama's rhetorical talents: "The sky will open, the light will come down, celestial choirs will be singing and everyone will know we should do the right thing."[1] Obama later conceded that this had been pretty funny, but he and his team were less amused by another attack in which she reminded voters not just of her own but also John McCain's greater experience: "I think you'll be able to imagine many things Senator McCain will be able to say—he's never been the president, but he will put forward his lifetime of experience....I will put forth my lifetime of experience. Senator Obama will put forth a speech he made in 2002."[2] Obama aides were furious that Clinton would help set up this talking point for the Republican to use in the event, increasingly likely, that Obama won the nomination.

The Clintons had their own gripe about partisan disloyalty. In a January 14, 2008, interview with the *Reno Gazette-Journal*, Obama had compared himself to the conservative icon Ronald Reagan:

> I don't want to present myself as some sort of singular figure. I think part of what's different are the times. I do think that, for example, the 1980 election was different. I think Ronald Reagan changed the trajectory of America in a way that, you know, Richard Nixon did not and in a way that Bill Clinton did not....He put us on a fundamentally different path because the country was ready for it....I think people just tapped into—he tapped into what people were already feeling, which was, we want clarity, we want optimism, we want a return to that sense of dynamism and entrepreneurship that had been missing.[3]

Obama clearly had given much thought to the Reagan example, which also appeared in his second book.[4] This may say something about Obama's view of the presidency, for Reagan was important as much or more for what he said as for what he did. The Reagan slogan "Morning in America" can be considered inspiring or corny, but as an observation about the sun coming up it was not something that one could credit a president with causing. Americans felt better about themselves and their country as economic conditions improved, yet the economic policies associated with Reagan—wrenching monetary contraction (the inflation-fighting work of Fed Chair Paul Volker, a Carter appointee) and expansive deficit spending (old-fashioned Keynesian policies dressed in conservatives' new supply-side clothing)—shaped but did not create the economic recovery of 1984. After a recession, *eventual* upswings in the business cycle are almost as inevitable as the rising sun.

Grander and quite implausible claims have been made for Reagan's role in ending the Cold War. The suggestion that he was largely responsible for "winning" it is hard to take seriously, given the foundations of containment that were laid down by seven administrations before him, and given the decisive factor of three Soviet general secretaries dying in a span of as many years, to be replaced by a genuinely reformist and increasingly radicalized Mikhail Gorbachev. Gorbachev already knew that the Soviet system, which he hoped to save, desperately required an exit from its stultifying dead end, and that the Cold War arms race made exit impossible. The Reagan (and Carter) increases in U.S. defense spending may have underlined this reality, but did not create it.[5]

A somewhat more plausible argument for Reagan's role is that he changed the moral discourse by speaking plainly. Early in his presidency Reagan called the Soviet Union an "evil empire" that would soon fall onto the "ash heap of history." Toward the end of his second term, Reagan stood at Berlin's Brandenburg Gate to implore, "Mr. Gorbachev, tear down this wall." Such language, it is argued, put America "on the right side of history," and there is something to this argument, so long as we appreciate its important limitations. The first limitation is that words alone do not drive events: the structural reasons for Gorbachev's reformism have already been stressed. Second, a more serious attention to the history reveals that Reagan's rhetoric reflected continuity as much as change from the preceding era: it was Carter before Reagan who pushed human rights to the center of American foreign policy discourse, and Ford before Carter who signed, together with the Soviets, the Helsinki Final Act containing human-rights pledges that proved surprisingly important as Communist bloc dissidents started to invoke them. Third, the clarity of Reagan's rhetoric and vision did not equate to an unyielding hard line. Reagan was ready, long before many of his hawk admirers, to trust Gorbachev's good intentions.[6] Being on the "right side of history" meant, crucially, being ready to grasp Gorbachev's outstretched hand. "Tear down this wall" was resonant not least because Reagan intuited that Gorbachev was just about ready to do so.

Along with Reagan, many have compared Obama to the slain Kennedy brothers: to Robert, for the high-voltage connection with adoring crowds and a moment in history;[7] to John, for an essential coolness and wit and seemingly easy eloquence. There are other points of comparison that are not uniformly positive. John F. Kennedy, three years younger in 1960 than Obama in 2008, struggled against perceptions that he was too young and not sufficiently experienced to lead America through Cold War crises. He also felt the need to convey sufficient toughness against the anticipated bullying of Soviet leader Nikita Khrushchev (and perhaps against the taint of appeasement associated with his father). And his inexperience, in fact, showed—most famously in the Bay of Pigs debacle. Khrushchev did bully him, moreover, in a face to face encounter at the Vienna summit that left Kennedy shaken and the country fearful.

In retrospect, moreover, and with Kennedy's presidency tragically unfinished, his admirers would never be able wholly to refute the suggestion that he triumphed more on the basis of style than substance. What *might have been* is unknowable, so the historian Robert Dallek suggests that we can assess only the Kennedy-*Johnson* government as a whole—as a full eight years that included Johnson's successful expansion of the welfare state and his civil rights legislation that effectively completed, after two centuries, the unfinished American Revolution.[8] (This Kennedy-Johnson legacy was itself diminished, of course, by the folly and tragedy of Vietnam.)

There is another answer to the charge about style over substance, which certainly applies to Kennedy and might have relevance for Obama. Kennedy's style—his wit and eloquence—seemed part of a capacity for insight that brought him to transcend, if not quite repudiate, the Cold Warrior toughness that was requisite to his times. This insight, a subjective imagination that brought him to consider the simple question of how things might appear from his opponent's viewpoint, was evident already in his inaugural address. "We shall pay any price, bear any burden," Kennedy famously said, "to assure the survival and the success of liberty." But in that snowy cold he also addressed a "request" to those "who would make themselves our adversary...that both sides begin anew the quest for peace, before the dark powers of destruction unleashed by science engulf all humanity in planned or accidental self-destruction."[9]

In the Cuban missile crisis, facing a choice of nuclear confrontation or appeasement, Kennedy in effect chose both. He faced down Khrushchev at the brink of nuclear annihilation, but he also rationally calculated the price of trading away U.S. missiles in Turkey to allow Khrushchev to save some face. Six months later, in his American University "peace speech"—what Dallek calls "one of the great state papers of any twentieth-century American presidency"[10]—Kennedy achieved perhaps the crowning moment of style as substance. The speech's visionary tone was tempered with sober realism. The visionary part, which is most remembered, was a plea that Americans and Russians should recognize their common humanity: "For in the final analysis, our most basic common link is that we all inhabit this small planet. We all breathe the same air. We all cherish our children's futures. And we are all mortal." But Kennedy also laid out a realistic path to this mutual recognition. His vision of coexistence, Kennedy insisted, was not the "absolute, infinite concept of universal peace and good will of which some fantasies and fanatics dream." It was, rather, "a more practical, more attainable peace, based not on a sudden revolution in human nature but on a gradual evolution in human institutions—on a series of concrete actions and effective agreements. . . . For peace is a process—a way of solving problems."

We know that this was a realistic vision for the simple reason that it came to pass. Kennedy's American University speech was an early part of the U.S. policy process that led to arms-control negotiations and détente with the Soviet Union. Contrary to neoconservative reading of history, it was this peace process that created the conditions—over two decades, with ups and downs, crises and setbacks, and a balance of annihilating military power always a factor—for the peaceful end of the Cold War.

Any consideration of the narrative impact of presidential speeches, however cursory, should include the president against whom Obama has so sharply defined himself. The George W. Bush presidency may seem notable mainly for deeds rather than words—for wars rather than speeches. Yet his words mattered greatly precisely because Bush and his subordinates strongly believed that words must have consequences; because they concluded, after September 11, that the framework in which Americans and their adversaries understood U.S. power had to be demolished and recast; and because they decided, apparently, that toppling the Taliban while leaving Saddam in power would be inadequate. Between the September 11 attacks and the invasion of Iraq, Bush and his speech writers were eloquent and admirably clear about the administration's intentions. American power could no longer crouch in a retaliatory posture. "The greater the threat, the greater the risk of inaction—and the more compelling the case for taking anticipatory action to defend ourselves, even if uncertainty remains as to the time and place of the enemy's attack."[11] And earlier in his *National Security Strategy* document: "History will judge harshly those who saw this coming danger but failed to act...the only path to peace and security is the path of action."[12] The requirement to prevent future threats with military force was inseparable, moreover, from the need to give practical effect to American ideals. The United States would therefore bolster and employ unmatchable military power to create "a balance of power that favors freedom."

In his second inaugural address, President Bush declared an American "ultimate goal of ending tyranny in our world." Five months later, in Cairo, Bush's new secretary of state, Condoleezza Rice, promised to break the pattern of "60 years" during which "my country, the United States, pursued stability at the expense of democracy in this region, in the Middle East, and we achieved neither....It is time," Rice continued, "to abandon the excuses that are made to avoid the hard work of democracy."[13]

By this point, however, the Bush administration had lost its audience. Whatever its true intentions, the U.S. invasion and occupation of Iraq was seen by most Arabs as the opposite of a war for freedom.[14] Even the more Machiavellian project of restoring respect for American power had manifestly failed. And Rice's vow that the United States would stop choosing expedience over the messy consequences of democracy failed its immediate test, when Hamas won decisively in January 2006 elections for the Palestinian parliament. The American policy response was international isolation and support for a Fatah coup against Hamas authority in Gaza. (That the coup failed was another embarrassment for self-styled Machiavellis.)

Though it is fair to say that he made things worse, President Bush cannot be blamed for the entire reservoir of Arab distrust about American designs. This reservoir was filled over generations: by the diversionary propaganda of undemocratic Arab regimes; by Arab cultural channels through which conspiracy theories flowed freely; and by real American blunders and problematic partnerships with oppressive governments. Rice was correct that democracy in the region was rarely, if ever, an American priority (though she may have gone overboard in supporting an Islamist narrative about American responsibility). The conviction of many Arabs that the central American purpose was to steal Arab oil was a cartoon caricature of an underlying truth: U.S. interests in the region included a secure supply of energy to fuel the world economy (this is not an especially selfish interest, but nor is it entirely selfless). American support for Israel was visceral and enduring; opposition to settlements was ineffectual; support for Palestinian statehood was belated and hedged.

To this unhappy narrative, President Bush added a policy of indefinitely detaining and sometimes torturing suspected terrorists—some of whom were innocent. His use of Manichean language to describe the war on terrorism made the U.S. response to 9/11 look like a Christian crusade. And the war he launched in Iraq could not possibly be explained to the Arab man on the street as a logical response to attacks by al Qaeda on America. (Incredulity on the Arab street was compounded, of course, when there turned out to be no active programs or supplies of chemical, biological, or nuclear weapons.) These policies, even in isolation, were ill-designed to win Arab support, but the key point is that they fed into a preestablished narrative of hostility and mistrust. Veteran U.S. diplomat James Dobbins has emphasized the unfortunate congruence in Arab minds between American occupation of Iraq and Israel's occupation of Palestinian territories. In January 2009, the month of transition between presidents Bush and Obama, Israel conducted military operations in Gaza. It was a defensive war, undertaken in response to rocket attacks against Israeli civilians. But it was also brutal in its effects on Gaza civilians. Four days before Obama's inauguration, one of the present authors walked across Cairo and listened at numerous backstreet mosques to the rage of Friday sermons: anguish for Gaza's "martyrs" and vitriol for their "Zionist" oppressors. This will be a hard story to untell.

A New Narrative?

One year into Obama's presidency, the argument that he was a man of fancy talk and limited accomplishment had been transmuted by conservatives into a rather more personal attack. Obama, they claimed, through hubris and excessive "self-regard," had overreached and—happily, from their perspective—failed in his attempt to shove an essentially center-right nation to the left.[15] In most respects, this was an odd accusation. That the president possesses abundant self-confidence is clear enough, but his critics have produced no real evidence for an unhealthy self-regard; indeed, the available evidence of modesty and civil exchanges with his political opponents points the other way.[16] The accusation of overreach requires an essential complacency about the trajectory that Obama inherited: a rejection of mainstream economists' near-consensus that without the massive stimulus package, economic depression was a real threat; indifference to the human costs of tens of millions without health insurance, including many whose preexisting conditions have made them uninsurable; a confidence that climate change does not pose a significant threat to our moral and strategic interests, despite the consensus of the U.S. intelligence community on this score. That the new president rejected complacency or resignation about these crises does not make him a radical leftist, or even overly ambitious.

There is, to be sure, one Obama conceit in which we believe him to be justified, but which is certainly open to debate. This is the idea that the narrative about America in much of the world, and especially in the Muslim world, had by 2008 become poisonous and significantly damaging to U.S. interests, but that it could also be corrected through a combination of words and deeds. *Narrative* is a word that has been occasionally discredited by the frivolity of some postmodern philosophy and literary criticism. Yet it is a word that we use often and without apology in this book, because we are convinced that the collective stories that societies tell about themselves and about others are significant factors in international history and relations. The U.S. administration and the president himself appear to believe this too. Before his inauguration, Obama aides let it be known that the new president intended to give a big speech early in his term in a Muslim capital and addressed to wider Muslim communities. He delivered the speech in Cairo, on June 4, 2009, and it was nothing if not audacious in its rhetorical ambitions:

> I've come here to Cairo to seek a new beginning between the United States and Muslims around the world....I do so recognizing that change cannot happen overnight. I know there's been a lot of publicity about this speech, but no single speech can eradicate years of mistrust, nor can I answer in the time that I have this afternoon all the complex questions that brought us to this point. But I am convinced that in order to move forward, we must say openly to each other the things we hold in our hearts and that too often are said only behind closed doors. There must be a sustained effort to listen to each other; to learn from each other; to respect one another; and to seek common ground.[17]

The language of the speech was both visionary and realistic. It was visionary insofar as it imagined that the peoples of the Middle East and the West—including Arabs, Israelis, Iranians, and Americans—can recognize in themselves and each other their common humanity. He drew on religious authority, citing the Koran, the Talmud, and the New Testament, and concluding: "The people of the world can live together in peace. We know that is God's vision. Now that must be our work here on Earth." It was realistic because it included at least the beginnings of a plausible work plan. The first step, said Obama, is to "say in public what we say in private" and to "act on what everyone knows to be true." Hence his focus on Israel's settlements in occupied territory:

Israelis must acknowledge that just as Israel's right to exist cannot be denied, neither can Palestine's. The United States does not accept the legitimacy of continued Israeli settlements. This construction violates previous agreements and undermines efforts to achieve peace. It is time for these settlements to stop.... Israel must also live up to its obligations to ensure that Palestinians can live, and work, and develop their society. And just as it devastates Palestinian families, the continuing humanitarian crisis in Gaza does not serve Israel's security; neither does the continuing lack of opportunity in the West Bank. Progress in the daily lives of the Palestinian people must be part of a road to peace, and Israel must take concrete steps to enable such progress.

Equally, he called on Arabs to admit publicly what they must know in their hearts: that Israel is here to stay, and that their own future is bound up with it. It was a plea to escape the trap of historical grievance that prevents everyone from recognizing and acting on their common interest for the future. Here, the resemblance to Kennedy's American University speech was significant. Kennedy had insisted that his vision was a practical one, "based not on a sudden revolution in human nature but on a gradual evolution in human institutions...."[18] Likewise, it was Obama's realist insight that the key to Middle East peace is not the triumph of democracy and virtue, much less the transformation of human hearts. Rather, a respect for contending historical narratives, and an end to bickering about who has suffered the most, is prerequisite to building on common interest.

Obama's bid for a general reconciliation between the United States and the world's Muslims included his specific outreach to Iran. The form of this outreach was not just controversial in the United States, but also fraught with moral and strategic dilemmas involving the confrontation between Iran's rulers and the emerging Green Movement.

The question of engagement had come out in stark terms during the long U.S. presidential campaign. During a July 2007 YouTube debate, Obama was asked, "Would you be willing to meet separately, without preconditions, during the first year of your Administration, in Washington or anywhere else, with the leaders of Iran, Syria, Venezuela, Cuba, and North Korea, in order to bridge the gap that divides our countries?" The candidate's response was a simple, "I would." The answer was seized on by Hillary Clinton as further evidence of the senator's dangerous inexperience. Obama's campaign aides were taken by surprise, worried, and discussing the next day how to walk the statement back, when Obama overheard them. As reported by the *New Yorker's* Ryan Lizza, the candidate told his aides "something to the effect of 'This is ridiculous. We met with Stalin. We met with Mao. The idea that we can't meet with Ahmadinejad is ridiculous.'"[19]

One of the assumptions against which he was battling holds that negotiating with tyrants helps legitimize them and thereby strengthens their rule. As Obama implied, however, the history of détente with the Soviets and the American opening to Mao's China also contains evidence for the opposite proposition: normalization of relations and relaxation of tensions can open up space for reformist and even dissident currents in and under repressive regimes.[20] In this regard, the case of Iran is particularly complex. Iranian popular opinion mixes desire for a more open society and some pro-American sentiment, on the one hand, with nationalist pride and wounded memories of U.S. intervention, on the other. The system itself is a surprising hybrid of democracy and theocracy. This was always an uneasy blend and, recent events suggest, an unsustainable one, because of centrality of the doctrine of *velayat e-faqih*—which gives a clerical Supreme Leader final say over all domestic and foreign policy matters.

This complexity is underscored by the events that unfolded in the run-up to and aftermath of the June 2009 elections. Ahmadinejad's first election in 2005 was part of a concerted reaction by a right wing bent on restoring the revolution to its proper trajectory in the wake of Mohammad Khatami's more liberal administration. The 2009 campaign gave hope to the liberals that they might reverse this reaction. During the weeks before the election Iranians witnessed an astonishingly open and spirited debate with opposition candidates complaining about the damage done to Iran's international reputation by the crude posturing of Ahmadinejad, including his forays into Holocaust denial and his belittling the seriousness of UN resolutions condemning Iran.[21]

There is some anecdotal evidence that Obama's offers of engagement, including his New Year's greeting and the Cairo speech, helped inspire this Tehran Spring. Mostly this is just speculation. Iranian students might very well have looked at Obama's own election as paradigmatic; if the much-demonized United States could elect such a different and attractive figure, why not hope for tectonic change in Iran? The Obama administration's disavowal of an American program of regime change arguably helped open the space for greater political debate about the pros and cons of Iran's foreign policy. Bernard Hourcade, a leading Western scholar of Iran who visits the country frequently, has argued that an American posture of "not interfering made it possible for nationalists to join the opposition."[22] David Menashri, an Iran-born professor of

Iranian studies at Tel Aviv University, said of the Green Movement protestors, "These are people who were indirectly encouraged by the emergence to the presidency of Barack H. Obama last November and adopted his call: 'Yes We Can.' This spirit of 'Obamaism' made the radical regime scared and concerned and gave the reformist elements heart and encouragement."[23]

Yet, although Obama might inspire, there were limits to his ability to help. Students might have been looking to the United States, but it is not clear what they were looking *for*. Nor could their leadership really tell them. These men—Hossein Mousavi, Mehdi Karroubi, and, even, to some extent, the former president and longtime power broker Ali Rafsanjani—were opposition leaders almost by default; they had stood as presidential candidates or, in the case of Rafsanjani, warned in advance against falsifying the results. Some religious authorities, including Ayatollah Hussein-Ali Montazeri, were longtime critics of the Islamic revolution's savage turn. But they were also long-standing Iranian elected officials and clerics with deep roots in the Islamic regime, unlikely to turn to the United States for legitimization or support.

Another awkward aspect was the strong possibility that Ahmadinejad actually won a majority of the votes cast. The *margin* of his official victory was preposterous, as was the speed with which it was announced; clearly, the supreme leader and other powers behind the president were unwilling to leave the outcome to the voters. Just as clearly, the Islamic Revolutionary Guards Corps exploited their subsequent brutal repression of the Green Movement in order to consolidate their power within the state. In this sense, the post-June events constituted another Persian irony: a right-wing coup to steal an election that the conservatives might have won anyway.

Against this background, the Obama administration's caution was both reasonable and problematic. It was reasonable to maintain as a first principle to do no harm, and to worry that an overt American embrace might discredit the opposition. It was problematic to "overlearn" the lessons of the Bush administration, in Nader Mousavizadeh's words, and to fail to leaven his realism with the deeply Obamaesque insight that narrative matters.[24] As the protest movement continued in the months after the elections, the regime's repression became more brutal. Security forces beat and sometimes fired on protestors, killing scores. Thousands were arrested, and many were tortured. Show trials ended with coerced confessions and death sentences. As of early February 2010, according to Human Rights Watch, 2 people had been put to death for "enmity with God," with another 10 sentenced to death for the same charge.[25] Eight days after the disputed election, President Obama vowed that "we will continue to bear witness" to the courage and defiance of Iranian protestors.[26] This—as his opponents pointed out—was not much, but then, there was really not much else he could do.

Message Fail

The day after Obama's Cairo speech, *New York Times* columnist David Brooks wrote approvingly of the Chicago-honed political skills that the new president was bringing to the Middle East.[27] "The Chicago mentality," in Brooks' formulation, referred to Obama's experience as a politician and community organizer mobilizing disparate groups on the basis of common, or at least overlapping, interests. Allusions to Chicago carry other connotations, however, including a certain targeted ruthlessness. Some of that would have been useful for the Obama administration's preparation and follow-through on the Cairo speech. The premise of the speech was that an American president was going to say what nobody in the past was willing to say, and the effect would be transformative. Measured in medium-term results, this did not happen.

Prior to the Cairo speech, according to a report by Laura Rozen on ForeignPolicy.com, Obama had sent letters to moderate Middle Eastern leaders in which he asked for modest "confidence building measures" to encourage Israel to agree to a settlement freeze.[28] The replies from both Jordan and Saudi Arabia were disappointing. Both governments reminded the president that they had already promised, in the "Arab Peace Initiative" of 2002, that a Palestinian-Israeli agreement, regardless of content, would result in diplomatic recognition of Israel by a broad front of Arab states. That would have to suffice as an incentive for Israel to negotiate constructively with Palestinian Arabs. Any additional steps, taken proactively by either Amman or Riyadh, would be pocketed by Israel and, at the end of the day, erode Jordanian and Saudi credibility.[29] Obama insisted that on his way to Cairo he would stop in Riyadh—a previously unplanned trip—to convince King Abdullah to be more forthcoming. Yet the *New York Times* was already reporting Saudi officials trying to wave off a visit by making it clear that whatever the president was asking for, the answer was going to be no. Since summits are customarily held to celebrate a prearranged "yes," one would have thought that the visit would have been scratched.[30] It went ahead only to show that, however powerful his oratory in Cairo, Arab leaders did not think Obama could deliver, and nor did they fear that they would pay a price for spurning him.[31]

The more serious mistake was to demand an Israeli settlements freeze without a plan for what to do if Israel said no. Washington's demand was loud and clear. The president "wants to see a stop to settlements—not some settlements, not outposts, not 'natural growth' exceptions" is how Secretary of State Clinton laid it out a few days before Cairo.[32] The Israeli refusal was just as adamant. Netanyahu may have sensed weakness in Obama's political position, or he may have been more concerned with his own political situation, since he was more vulnerable to a challenge from the right than from any other quarter. The result was a major defeat for the U.S. administration, and for the Palestinians who depended on it. Palestinian president Mahmoud Abbas told *Asharq al Awsat*: "Obama laid down the condition of halting the settlements completely. What could I say to him? Should I say this is too much?"[33]

In a fallback, the administration explored various compromises with Netanyahu, settling for a temporary halt to new residential construction in Palestinian areas of the West Bank. Israel said it would stop building for 10 months, but would complete about 2,900 units for which permits had already been granted. East Jerusalem was exempted.

After Obama's ringing declaration in Cairo that "settlements must stop," this was considered pretty weak tea, and derided by Arabs as a defeat for an administration that had never been really serious about putting the arm on Israel. Secretary Clinton transformed Arab derision to mockery by saying, "What the prime minister [Netanyahu] has offered in specifics on restraints on a policy of settlements...is unprecedented."[34] This was technically true, but as the outcome of a six-month struggle intended to reframe the Israeli-Palestinian peace process, it seemed meager and dispiriting. The fight had been bruising. Arabs and Israelis had both lost at least some confidence in Obama's skill, determination, and dedication to principle.

"We won a lot of credibility in the Arab world with the settlements stand," a high-level administration official told us, "and it eroded just as quickly."[35] It may be the case that the excitement of an historical moment engendered some overconfidence on the Obama team. For one thing, they could observe a genuine change in U.S. politics regarding Israel and imagine that it gave them more leverage over Jerusalem than it actually delivered. The genuine change was a palpable widening of the spectrum of debate about U.S. support for Israeli policies. To understand this change, it is necessary to be clear about preexisting conditions. Senators and House members who criticized Israel often found themselves facing a well-funded reaction, such that it was easy to conclude that it just wasn't worth the trouble.[36] The American Jewish community, small but politically active, was predominantly liberal but prone to give Israel the benefit of the doubt on security matters. This tendency was magnified by the fact that, after Oslo, Jewish organizations' leaderships at the national level became more conservative. The former liberal leadership cadre moved on to lobby for a progressive domestic social and economic agenda once the Oslo process was underway and a more conservative religious elite—for whom Oslo did not signify progress—took its place at the forefront of the pro-Israel lobby. These more conservative Jewish leaders were able to magnify their influence by joining forces with the newly ascendant Christian Right.

The recent change has been a subtle reaction against this conservative orthodoxy. The overwhelming Jewish vote for Obama over McCain should not have surprised, given the liberal traditions of Jewish voters, but it did happen in the face of a fierce campaign to convince Jews that Obama was hostile to Israel. After his May 2009 visit to Washington, Prime Minister Netanyahu was reportedly "flummoxed by an unusually united line [on the settlements freeze] that has come not just from the Obama White House and the secretary of state, but also from pro-Israel congressmen and women who have come through Israel for meetings with him over Memorial Day recess."[37] The institutional expression of this new mood was the establishment of J-Street, a mainly Jewish-funded, pro-peace lobbying group with the declared mission of countering more conservative and Likud-oriented pro-Israel groups.

Israeli governments should probably recognize these developments as significant and lasting. But those of us hoping for a more critical form of U.S. support for Israel must also recognize that if there is a sea change, it is largely confined to the American center-left. This is political territory from which only a politically powerful president can sustain a foreign policy that departs significantly—regarding Israel and other matters—from pre-established and well-worn tracks. It is not so much that America is a "center-right nation" in terms of voters' policy preferences, though U.S. polling does find more self-styled "conservatives" than "liberals." More important is the fact that the American system skews right, as in a U.S. Senate that disproportionately favors rural, conservative interests, and where the Republican minority decided to compound that disproportion by mounting routine filibusters against Obama's entire legislative agenda. The U.S. president was already palpably weakened by high unemployment creating a sour electorate. Legislative gridlock inspired predictions of a failed presidency. The Israeli press reported that Netanyahu was heartened by news from America that the president's ambitious health-care reforms were in trouble.[38] Obama's subsequent triumph in bringing health reform back from the dead suggested, conversely, a stronger position from which to confront the Israeli government.

But these political wins and losses are only relative as sources of foreign policy authority. The fundamental problem facing Obama is a Republican opposition that has fallen back on cliché and demagoguery instead of seriously grappling with the dilemmas of America's world role. Most egregious is the Republicans' and right-wing media's determined campaign against President Obama's effort to reaffirm and reestablish an American consensus against torture.

For Netanyahu, locked into a right-wing coalition with religious parties as well as Avigdor Lieberman's Yisrael Beiteinu party, which endorses continued occupation of the West Bank, there will be repeated temptations to join forces with the American right in tacit alliance against Obama. Obama officials who served in the Clinton administration have bitter memories of Netanyahu when he last headed a Likud government in the 1990s doing something similar against Bill Clinton. Fighting off Clinton's pressure for more accommodating Israeli policies, Netanyahu consorted with right-wing Christian Zionists such as Jerry Falwell—who at the time was peddling videos accusing the U.S. president of murder. Clinton in the late 1990s was far more popular among Israelis than Obama in 2010. The Israeli government might hope to ride out his presidency, perhaps even helping to limit it to one term. But this, it seems to us, would be a mistake on at least two levels. First, although the American center-left will not turn anti-Israeli in any commonsensical meaning of the term, its further alienation from Israel's governing politicians would not constitute a net gain for Israel's relationship with its most important ally. More fundamentally, an American right that encourages further Israeli intransigence is not offering any realistic solutions to Israel's long-term dilemmas.

Of course, to sell his own solutions, and at the same time recast America's relations with the world's Muslims, President Obama will be required, at the same time, to better navigate the currents of Israeli public opinion. Many Israelis clearly mistrust Obama. Polling in midsummer 2009 indicated that only 6 percent of Israelis felt Obama was a strong supporter of Israel.[39] Subsequent surveys have shown him to have recovered to a level of greater popularity than most Israeli politicians and institutions, but that is not a very high standard. Obama's Cairo speech not only took Israel to task for settlement expansion, but also justified Israel's existence to his Arab audience as a consequence of the Holocaust, rather than, as Israelis prefer to see it, an historic claim to the land described in the Hebrew Bible and actualized in continuous Israelite or Jewish residence even after the bulk of the Jewish population was deported by Roman imperial edict in the first century CE. From an Israeli perspective, the U.S. president's appeal came unpleasantly close to convergence with the Arab reading of Zionist history, in which the establishment of Israel by colonial powers was a maneuver to assuage European guilt at the expense of Palestine's autochthonous Arab population.

This is not, of course, what Obama intended. When White House officials were pressed on this point, they stressed the passages in the Cairo speech that voiced an unshakable U.S. commitment to Israel, rejection of violence as a legitimate form of resistance, and disdain for the instrumentalization of anti-Zionism by authoritarian Arab regimes.[40] Moreover, it should also be obvious that American association with *biblical* claims to the land of Zion will only deepen the convictions of many Muslims that they are under assault in a civilizational conflict and religious war. Of course, many Americans do think in biblical terms and the Israelis do have a biblical history in Palestine that is supported by archaeological and literary evidence that is not seriously disputed by Western, non-Jewish scholars. Yet it requires no special expertise to understand that perceptions of a civilizational war serve the purposes of al Qaeda and other violent jihadists, especially when fueled by disinformation about what Israelis are up to, as in vigorously disseminated stories about Israel's rebuilding of the Temple. It is therefore counterproductive for right-wing American politicians to promote just this narrative. This became evident with the political rise of "Christian Zionism," a potent force in American politics in which God's biblical promise of Palestine to the people of Israel carries great weight. Also important is the belief that at the end of history a great battle will be fought in what is now Israel, and that this cataclysmic confrontation will require the participation of the Jews. The state of Israel is therefore an essential validation of scriptural history and a vital prerequisite for Christian redemption. The American religious right opposed the Oslo peace process and scrutinized George W. Bush administration policy statements on Israel for signs that the White House was pressing the Israelis to abandon their territorial claims in the West Bank and Gaza. More recently, past and possibly future Republican candidates Mike Huckabee and Sarah Palin have been among the most vocal in arguing for an Israeli Jewish right to settle in the occupied territories.[41]

William Kristol and other U.S. conservatives have pointed to and celebrated shared religiosity as an important American-Israeli link (and one that distinguishes both countries from more secular European societies).[42] There is, to be sure, much to admire in the religious devotion of many Americans and Israelis. But when this piety is expressed as opposition to dividing the land of historic Palestine, it can bring nothing but trouble.

A more promising strand of shared Israeli-American narrative—one that avoids both religious absolutism and the lachrymose storytelling that hinges on the continuity of Jewish suffering—would focus on the 1948 war, when Jews fought successfully for survival and their own state. Of course, this event is remembered as a "catastrophe"— *al-Nakba* in Arabic—by Arabs and other Muslims. But it has the virtue of embodying a secular struggle—warfare—that is logically followed by some form of peace. The fruits of war may be bitter, but they are rarely nonnegotiable. This is what distinguishes a secular war from a religious crusade.

In any event, the notion that the trauma of the Holocaust can be stricken from international understanding of and support for Israel's right to exist is not very realistic. No Israeli would be oblivious to the role of the Holocaust in complicating Britain's ability to enforce Jewish immigration quotas prior to independence or in winning U.S. recognition for the new Jewish state. Current Israeli leaders, as we have seen, are hardly hesitant about invoking the Holocaust to warn of Iranian and other threats to the Jewish homeland. American politicians of both left and right regularly do the same, along with European—especially German—opinion makers. It would be surprising if they did not, since the European Holocaust plays such a central role in the West's collective historiography.

Another factor that Israelis may need to understand is that Obama's operating mode, although manifestly inspiring, is at the same time cool and cerebral, whether he is talking about the economy, health-care reform, or war in Afghanistan. That there was, after Cairo, no follow-up presidential visit to Israel and none of the sentimentality of the Clinton era, or the comrades-in-arms posturing of the Bush administration, compounded fears that the U.S. president was not in Israel's corner. Much of this cannot be helped—President Obama's unsentimental eye for things is both a virtue and vice.

Obama's confrontation with Israel's government was hardened during Vice President Joe Biden's March 2010 visit to Israel by another episode in the settlements dispute. The gregarious Biden, more popular in Israel than the president, was sent by Obama to help repair relations with a reaffirmation of America's "iron-clad" commitment to Israel's security. He was greeted with the news that Israel's housing ministry had approved the construction of 1,600 new housing units in mainly Arab East Jerusalem. The administration reacted furiously, with Obama himself directing Biden's condemnation of the decision in a Tel Aviv speech, and instructing Secretary Clinton to demand a reversal of the approvals in a tense, 45-minute phone conversation with the Israeli prime minister. Netanyahu apologized for the timing, saying it had caught him by surprise, but refused to budge on the substance. The standoff suggested the worst crisis in U.S.-Israeli relations for at least two decades.[43]

The Americans' anger was justified.[44] Eventually, however, and without changing his position on settlements or the peace process, Obama will need to better connect with an Israeli audience. As Aluf Benn, the dean of Israel's diplomatic correspondents, put it in a *cri de coeur* in the *New York Times*:

> Perhaps there are good reasons behind Mr. Obama's Middle East policy. Perhaps the settlement freeze is in Israel's best interest. Perhaps the president is truly committed to Israel's long-term security and wellbeing. Perhaps his popularity in the Arab street is the missing ingredient of peacemaking. But until the president talks to us, we won't know. Next time you're in the neighborhood, Mr. President, speak to us directly. We will surely listen.[45]

Containing the Crisis

This may be necessary not least if the United States wants to forestall an Israeli attack on Iran. We have criticized Israel in this book, but we have also made clear our view that a war between Israel and Iran is not something that Israel seeks. War, if it comes, will be a tragic consequence of Iran's recklessness and Israel's fears. But war would also be, under most scenarios we can envision, a tragic mistake. The possible upside can be expressed in two sentences. An Israeli attack that significantly degraded Iran's nuclear weapons capability might conceivably benefit counterproliferation objectives, the integrity of the NPT regime, and the compliance of member states with meaningful inspection arrangements. The use of force against Iran's nuclear program would, at a minimum, show that attempts to exploit the restraint of interested powers, manipulate the diplomatic process, game the NPT, and impede International Atomic Energy Agency (IAEA) access to nuclear-related facilities can carry serious penalties. But the likely damage to U.S.—and, by extension,

Israeli—interests from an Israeli attack, even if operationally successful, would probably outweigh the benefits.

First, regardless of perceptions of U.S. complicity in the attack, the United States would probably become embroiled militarily in any Iranian retaliation against Israel or other countries in the region. Given uncertainties about the future of Iraq and a deepening commitment to Afghanistan, hostilities with Iran would stretch U.S. military capabilities at a particularly difficult time, while potentially derailing domestic priorities. Second, an Israeli strike would cause oil prices to spike and heighten concerns that energy supplies throughout the Persian Gulf might become disrupted. Should Iran attempt to block the Strait of Hormuz by mining, cruise missile strikes, or small boat attacks, these fears would be realized, at least for a short period. Third, since the United States would be viewed as having assisted Israel, Washington's desire to woo the Muslim world would almost certainly be thwarted. A setback in the struggle against jihadist terrorism is a likely consequence. Fourth, although some argue that the popular anger aroused in Iran by a strike would be turned against a discredited clerical regime that seemed to invite foreign attack after its bloody postelection repression of a nonviolent opposition, it is more likely that Iranians of all stripes would rally around the flag. If so, the opposition Green Movement would be undermined, while the ascendant hard-line clerics and Revolutionary Guard supporters would face fewer constraints in consolidating their hold on power. Fifth, if Tehran is undecided about whether to go for actual weaponization, an Israeli attack will no doubt push it in that direction. Sixth, although progress toward an Israeli-Palestinian final status accord is already elusive, an Israeli strike, especially one that overflew Jordan or Saudi Arabia, would delay fruitful renewed negotiation indefinitely. Both Washington and Jerusalem would be too preoccupied with managing the consequences of an attack, while regional capitals would continue to deflect U.S. appeals to upgrade relations with Israel as an incentive to concessions. If Hamas or Hezbollah were to retaliate against Israel, either spontaneously or in response to Iranian pressure to act, any revival of the peace process would be further set back, especially if fighting in Lebanon spread to Syria. Finally, depending on the circumstances surrounding an Israeli attack, the political-military relationship between Jerusalem and Washington could fray, which would erode unity among Democrats and embolden Republicans, thereby complicating the administration's political situation, and weaken Israel's deterrent. Even if an Israeli move on Iran did not dislocate the bilateral relationship, it could instead produce diplomatic rifts between the United States and its European and regional allies, reminiscent of tensions over the Iraq war. Not all of these consequences are likely to converge simultaneously; a few would be enough to make an Israeli strike problematic.

To prevent these outcomes, the United States will need to construct a credible regime of containment, including sufficient reassurance in the form of strengthened military protection and guarantees for Israel and Arab states. As noted in chapter 3, this is already happening with arms sales, expanded bases and naval presence, and missile defenses for countries deemed targets of Iranian threats.[46] Diplomacy to persuade Iran to limit its nuclear program will no doubt continue; if the results continue to disappoint, tougher sanctions will be inevitable. Sanctions, as noted in chapter 4, are usually only symbolic in effect and can be, in some respects, counterproductive. Still, the symbolism may be required, to indicate international disapproval of Iran's behavior, and to reassure Israel that the problem is not forgotten. Sanctions can play a role, moreover, along with sabotage that is apparently ongoing, in slowing Iran's nuclear progress.

If pressure and diplomacy to stop Iran's nuclear program fail, U.S. security guarantees to Israel and the Arabs will have to become clearer. Explicit *nuclear* guarantees are probably unnecessary and could be counterproductive, not least because they would run counter to the administration's policy of deemphasizing the role of nuclear weapons. But Washington can make clear that Iran's use of nuclear weapons would trigger an overwhelming American retaliation through whatever means were necessary to guarantee the destruction and demise of Iran's ruling regime.

Israel, of course, has its own nuclear deterrent force. Whether the supplement of such an American security guarantee will be sufficient to restrain Israel from attacking, or Arab states from developing their own nuclear programs, is hard to say. In principle, however, we believe that such guarantees *should be* sufficient. We say this fully aware of the caveats, dangers, and uncertainties of deterrence. But these uncertainties have adhered to other deterrence arrangements as well. The Iranian challenge is not fundamentally different from those; certainly there is no evidence that Iran's regime is less rational than the Soviet Union under Stalin or China during the Cultural Revolution. As veteran U.S. diplomat James Dobbins, one of the few Americans with recent experience in negotiating with Iranians, put it, "The [Iranian] leadership doesn't compare to Mao and Stalin. Both were psychopaths by the time they had developed nuclear weapons."[47]

A successful regime of containment will also have to include a readiness, under certain circumstances, for U.S.

military action, with support and possibly participation of key allies such as Britain and France, against Iran's nuclear facilities or other targets. Such a prescription is of course in tension with, but does not contradict, our earlier warnings about the damaging consequences of military action. We oppose the military option under most circumstances. But there might be circumstances in which the baleful consequences of inaction outweigh the terrible consequences of war. A purpose of the containment regime should be to enforce a redline before weaponization, nuclear testing, or withdrawal from the NPT. Whether Tehran's crossing of that line should require a military response is not something we can say with confidence, because it would depend on attending circumstances. A mildly reformist Iran, that had toned down its rhetoric against Israel and curtailed its active support for Hezbollah, Hamas, and other terrorists, would pose a different kind of challenge in crossing that redline than would a belligerent and unrestrained Iran. There is a spectrum of scenarios in between these extremes. In any event, the military option will not and should not be taken off the table. And the possibility of Israel going down that road, even against the wishes of Washington, is an objective reality that has been discussed, at length, in this book.

The containment regime we are describing entails, in many respects, an augmented U.S. military and strategic commitment to the Middle East. This is problematic for a United States that seeks withdrawal from Iraq and anticipates a drawdown from Afghanistan after the current surge has unfolded, and that has become more attentive to the fiscal and economic burdens of its overseas commitments.[48] It is also problematic because America's previous penetrations into the Middle East have provoked various forms of reaction, including the attacks of September 11,

2001, which can be traced to the vast U.S. deployment of forces to Saudi Arabia a decade before. There is a case to be made for America to adopt an "over-the-horizon" posture for the region. This is not likely to happen, however. So it is all the more a fundamental American interest to resolve or at least see progress toward resolving the Palestinians' plight, a moral and strategic hemorrhage for both the United States and Israel. In 2009, President Obama called for a complete halt to Israeli settlement construction as the most immediate and tangible way to show such progress. That Obama made tactical, even serious, mistakes in this regard does not obscure the truth that, on the substance of the matter, he was right and successive Israeli governments have been wrong. Martin Indyk, a former White House Middle East adviser, ambassador to Israel, and vigorous advocate of a U.S.-Israeli special relationship, put it starkly at the time of Obama's inauguration, when he said that unrestrained settlement activity and Palestinian terrorism, while "not moral equivalents...are equivalent in the damage they have done to the hope of peace and the viability of a two-state solution."[49] Israel naturally will make its own decisions, constrained, to a considerable extent, by the requirements of coalition politics. But if it chooses, or feels compelled, to ignore American interests on the matter, it will make America's position in the greater Middle East all the more difficult.[50]

Concepts of containment must also reflect realistic thinking about the future of Iran. Analogies to Cold War containment of the Soviets are inexact and inherently flawed, but there are some points of comparison. The Iranian state is repressive, yet in many respects Iranian politics have been pluralistic, and Iranian society is both traumatized and hopeful. We cannot predict how the conflicts within Iran's society and regime will evolve, let alone whether the unfolding of these conflicts will yield opportunities for U.S. diplomacy in resolving the nuclear crisis. We have not seen any convincing arguments about how the United States or other outside powers can affect the outcome of political struggles there, except perhaps on the margins. Still, the rise of the Green Movement and the dramatic events since the June 2009 elections do suggest that some of the principles of Cold War containment, as set forth at the outset by George F. Kennan, are relevant to the developing confrontation with Iran. Build up strength and resilience in our allies rather than seeking recklessly to destroy our opponents. Keep the moral high ground and keep our nerve. Contain challenges against us "by the adroit and vigilant application of counter-force" and be ready to follow up with diplomacy.[51] Do not go off half-cocked into ill-considered wars without understanding whom we are fighting, or how.

If these principles are applied with prudence and historical patience, it seems reasonable to look forward to a "mellowing," if not the radical reform of an Iranian regime that, like the Soviet Union, is riddled with contradiction. Such a development, along with progress resolving the conflict between Israel and Palestinians, would considerably lighten if not completely end America's strategic burden in the region.

There is much to hope for in this, but also much that can go wrong. Goodwill and determination are necessary but not sufficient conditions for successful American strategies. At the outset, this book identified six central crises in America's post–World War II encounter with the Middle East. It was the third crisis—the Iranian revolution—that did much to destroy an American presidency. This was after President Jimmy

Carter, unnaturally stubborn and religiously devoted to his own vision of peace, brokered a treaty between Israel and Egypt that has endured for three decades. Yet Carter was soon overwhelmed by a perfect storm of converging disasters, and it has even been suggested that his immersion in the Arab-Israeli peacemaking rendered his administration deaf to the storm warnings in Iran.[52]

And while few today would look at Barack Obama and see Jimmy Carter, the current crises are more or less direct descendents of those that did in Carter. The Iranian Islamists who took Carter's diplomats hostage are now building a nuclear capability. The jihadist war that was set off by the Soviet invasion of Afghanistan is now killing American troops, and threatens the future of nuclear-armed Pakistan. The 1970s inflation and unemployment that ended America's postwar boom has now been matched by the most rapid collapse of economic demand since the Great Depression. The oil shocks of 1973 and 1978 would almost surely recur in a war that blocked the Strait of Hormuz. In fact, the oil crisis of the 1970s has risen to an existential level, because the problem of energy security is now inextricably linked to the environmental crisis of the twenty-first century.

The compressed coil of disaster linking Iran, Israel, and the United States is not the only problem facing the Obama administration, and it may not even be its worst problem. But Iran's defiance and Israel's panic are the fuses for a war that could destroy all of Obama's other ambitions. The sixth crisis could shape our world for many years to come.

Notes

Introduction

1. "In Crisis, Opportunity for Obama," WSJ.com (November 21, 2008), http://online.wsj.com/article/SB122721278056345271.html.

2. Readers may query why we have not included in this list the 1948 Arab-Israeli war through which Israel achieved statehood. Although obviously crucial for what followed in the Middle East, the 1948 war was not a crisis for the United States in the sense of confronting Washington with particularly difficult choices or policy dilemmas. There *was* a debate in the US government, with Secretary of State George Marshall arguing that recognition of Israel would hurt American interests in the Arab world. However, President Truman's decision to support Israel was never really in doubt. Moreover, Moscow's immediate recognition of Israeli independence neutralized the Cold War relevance of the conflict until some years later, and the Haganah (predecessor of the Israeli Defense Forces) received most of its weapons from the Eastern bloc. The war foreshadowed but did not immediately require an American strategic commitment.

3. "Iran Leader Urges Destruction of 'Cancerous' Israel," CNN.com (December 15, 2000); available at http://archives.cnn.com/2000/WORLD/meast/12/15/mideast.iran.reut/. Yossi Melman, 'Ahmadinejad: Israel is 'rotten tree that will be anihilated,' *Haaretz* (June 16 2006), http://www.haaretz.com/print-edition/news/ahmadinejad-israel-is-rotten-tree-that-will-be-annihilated-1.185329; 'Iran's President Reiterates Threat Against Israel' *Associated Press* (April 15 2006), http://www.washingtonpost.com/wp-dyn/content/article/2006/04/14/AR2006041401471.html.

4. Authors' conversation with David Menashri, Tel Aviv, July 2009.

5. News Conference by President Obama, Palaiz de la Musique et Des Congres, Strasbourg, France (April 2, 2009), http://www.whitehouse.gov/the_press_office/News-Conference-By-President-Obama-4-04–2009.

6. For example, Karl Rove, "The President's Apology Tour," *Wall Street Journal* (April 23, 2009), http://online.wsj.com/article/SB124044156269345357.html; Charles Krauthammer, "It's Your Country Too Mr. President," *Washington Post* (April 10, 2009), http://www.washingtonpost.com/wp-dyn/content/article/2009/04/09/AR2009040903367.html?hpid=opinionsbox1.

7. "Remarks by the President on a New Beginning," Cairo University, Cairo, Egypt (June 4, 2009), http://www.whitehouse.gov/the_press_office/Remarks-by-the-President-at-Cairo-University-6-04–09/.

Chapter 1

1. Ray Takeyh, *Guardians of the Revolution—Iran and the World in the Age of the Ayatollahs* (New York: Oxford University Press, 2009), 212.

2. The U.S. President George W. Bush's State of the Union Address, Washington, D.C. (January 29, 2002), http://georgewbush-whitehouse.archives.gov/news/releases/2002/01/20020129-11.html.

3. One might add that both the United States and Iran had supported the Muslim government in Bosnia against Croatian and espe-

cially Serb attacks. It must be stressed, however, that Iran had very different goals in Bosnia than the United States. Although the Clinton administration tacitly approved copious arms shipments from Iran to Bosnia, in contravention of a UN arms embargo, it was alarmed about and pressured the Bosnian government to curtail IRGC and other mujahideen activities there. Daniel Williams and Thomas W. Lippman, "US Is Allowing Iran to Arm Bosnia Muslims," *Washington Post*, April 14, 1995; author interview with then U.S. defense secretary William Perry, February 1996.

4. James Dobbins, *After the Taliban—Nation-Building in Afghanistan* (Washington D.C: Potomac Books, 2008), 142–143.

5. Mark Fitzpatrick, *The Iranian Nuclear Crisis: Avoiding Worst-Case Outcomes, Adelphi Paper 398* (London: Routledge, 2008), 11–20; *IISS Military Balance 2009*, vol. 109 (London: Routledge, 2009), 233. See also chapter on Iran's ballistic missile program in IISS Strategic Dossier on Iran (2005), 87–108.

6. Since 2006, the UN Security Council has approved four resolutions under Chapter VII of the UN Charter, regarding Iran's nuclear program. Most Chapter VII resolutions determine the existence of a threat to the peace, a breach of the peace, or an act of aggression in accordance with Article 39. Qualifying an event as a threat to "international peace and security" entitles the council to make recommendations or decide what measures (including, but not restricted to, the use of force) can be taken to redress the threat. See Michael J. Matheson, *Council Unbound: The Growth of UN Decision Making on Conflict and Postconflict Issues after the Cold War* (Washington DC: United States Institute of Peace, 2006) and http://www.un.org/en/documents/charter/chapter7.shtml for Chapter VII articles.

7. Fareed Zakaria, "The Arrogant Empire," *Newsweek* (March 24, 2003), http://www.newsweek.com/id/59792/page/1.

8. Text of President Bush's speech to the 57th UN General Assembly, *VOA News* (September 12, 2002), http://www1.voanews.com/english/news/a-13-a-2002-09-12-32-Text-67581067.html?moddate=2002-09-12.

9. David Hannay, "Three Iraq Intelligence Failures Reconsidered," *Survival* 51, no. 6 (December 2009–January 2010): 16.

10. "Casual Conversations with SSA George Piro," (June 11, 2004), 2, U.S. Department of Justice, FBI, Baghdad Operations Center, http://www.gwu.edu/~nsarchiv/NSAEBB/NSAEBB279/24.pdf.

11. Bob Drogin, "The Vanishing," *New Republic* (July 21, 2003), http://www.tnr.com/article/the-vanishing.

12. Maziar Bahari, "118 Days, 12 Hours, 54 Minutes," *Newsweek* (November 30, 2009), http://www.newsweek.com/id/223862/page/1.

13. Iran: Nuclear Intentions and Capabilities, NIE (November 2007), available at http://www.dni.gov/press_releases/20071203_release.pdf.

14. Author interviews with U.S. intelligence analysts, January 2008.

15. Henry A. Kissinger, "Misreading the Iran Report: Why Spying and Policymaking Don't Mix," *The Washington Post* (December 13, 2007), http://www.washingtonpost.com/wp-dyn/content/article/2007/12/12/AR2007121202331.html.

16. Thomas Fingar, "Remarks and Q&A by the Deputy Director of National Intelligence for Analysis & Chairman, National Intelligence Council," Commonwealth Club, San Francisco, California (February 14, 2008), http://www.dni.gov/speeches/20080214_speech.pdf.

17. Author interview with U.S. intelligence analyst, Washington DC, Nov. 2009.

18. *IISS Military Balance 2009*, vol. 109 (London: Routledge, 2009), 233. See chapter on Iran's ballistic missile program in IISS Strategic Dossier on Iran (2005), 87–108.

19. Fareed Zakaria, "They May Not Want the Bomb, and Other Unexpected Truths," *Newsweek* (June 1, 2009), http://www.newsweek.com/id/199147. It is of course easy to imagine that Iran's clerics could issue a new fatwa at a critical moment pronouncing that new threats to Iran make nuclear weapons religiously permissible.

20. E-mail to author from Iraq expert Toby Dodge, relating his interview with Tariq Aziz in Baghdad, September 11, 2002.

21. This evidence includes drawings, computer simulations of warhead detonations, and documents detailing Iranian work on shaping uranium for nuclear cores and conventional trigger mechanisms for nuclear detonations. Fitzpatrick, *Iranian Nuclear Crisis*, 15–17.

22. David Sanger and William J. Broad, "Inspectors Say Iran Worked on a Warhead," *New York Times* (February 18, 2010), http://www.nytimes.com/2010/02/19/world/middleeast/19iran.html.

23. Sam Gardiner quoted in James Fallows, "The Nuclear Power beside Iraq," *Atlantic* (May 2006), http://www.theatlantic.com/doc/200605/fallows-iran/2.

24. National Security Directive (NSDD 139) from Ronald W. Reagan. "Measures to Improve U.S. Posture and Readiness to Respond to Developments in the Iran-Iraq War" (April 5, 1984), 3, http://www.gwu.edu/~nsarchiv/NSAEBB/NSAEBB82/iraq53.pdf.

25. Department of State Cable from George P. Shultz to the United States Embassy in Sudan. "Briefing Notes for Rumsfeld Visit to Baghdad," March 24, 1984, http://www.gwu.edu/~nsarchiv/NSAEBB/NSAEBB82/iraq48.pdf; see also Christopher Marquis, "Rumsfeld Made Iraq Overture in &rlenis;84 Despite Chemical Raids," *New York Times* (December 23, 2003), http://www.nytimes.com/2003/12/23/international/middleeast/23RUMS.html?pagewanted=1

26. Shahram Chubin, "Iran and the War: From Stalemate to Ceasefire," in Efraim Karsh, *The Iran/Iraq War: Impact and Implications* (London: Macmillan Press, 1987), 21.

27. Takeyh, *Guardians of the Revolution,* 105.

28. See Donald W. Riegle Jr., "U.S. Chemical and Biological Warfare-Related Dual Use Exports to Iraq and Their Possible Impact on the Health Consequences of the Gulf War," Committee on Banking, Housing and Urban Affairs (May 25, 1994), http://www.gulfweb.org/bigdoc/report/r_1_2.html#exports, and U.S. Senate Banking Committee, "Second Staff Report on U.S. CBW-Related Dual-Use Exports to Iraq" (May 25, 1994), http://www.gulfwarvets.com/arison/banking.htm. Tom Drury, "How Iraq Built Its Weapons Programs, with a Little Help from Its Friends," *St. Petersburg Times* (March 16, 2003), http://www.sptimes.com/2003/03/16/Perspective/How_Iraq_built_its_we.shtml.

29. Takeyh, *Guardians of the Revolution,* p. 104.

30. Steven M. Walt, "Revolution and War," *World Politics* 44, no. 3 (April 1992): 321–368; http://www.jstor.org/stable/2010542.

31. Lawrence Freedman, *A Choice of Enemies: America Confronts the Middle East* (London: Weidenfeld & Nicholson, 2008), 18.

32. President Jimmy Carter's State of the Union Address, Washington D.C. (January 23, 1980), http://www.jimmycarterlibrary.org/documents/speeches/su8ojec.phtml.

33. Freedman, *Choice of Enemies*, 72, 79.

34. Thomas Friedman, *From Beirut to Jerusalem* (London: Collins, 1990); Robert C. McFarlane, "From Beirut to 9/11," *New York Times* (October 22, 2008), http://www.nytimes.com/2008/10/23/opinion/23mcfarlane.html?_r=2&oref=slogin.

35. Charles Krauthammer, "Only in Their Dreams," *Time* (December 2001), http://www.time.com/time/magazine/article/0,9171,1101011224–188565,00.html; George P. Shultz, "Terrorism and the Modern World," *U.S. State Department Bulletin* (December 1984), http://findarticles.com/p/articles/mi_m1079/is_v84/ai_3536847/pg_3/?tag=content;col1.

36. Murray S. Waas and Craig Unger, "Annals of Government: In the Loop, Bush's Secret Mission," *New Yorker* (November 2, 1992), http://www.newyorker.com/archive/1992/11/02/1992_11_02_064_TNY_CARDS_000359993.

37. "Iran's Leader Challenges U.S. and Talks of Re-Election Bid," *New York Times* (February 1, 1993), http://www.nytimes.com/1993/02/01/world/iran-s-leader-challenges-us-and-talks-of-re-election-bid.html?pagewanted=1.

38. Mehrdad Valibeigi, "US-Iranian Trade Relations After the Revolution," in *Post Revolutionary Iran*, ed. Hooshang Amirahmadi and Manoucher Parvin (Boulder, Colo.: Westview, 1988).

39. Richard A. Clarke, *Against All Enemies: Inside America's War on Terror* (New York: Free Press, 2004), 120–129.

40. "America and Iran: Mutual Incomprehension," *IISS Strategic Comments* 9, no. 6 (August 2003): 1–2. Available online at http://www.informaworld.com/smpp/content~db=all~content=a768140559.

41. Barbara Slavin, *Bitter Friends, Bosom Enemies: Iran, the U.S. and the Twisted Path to Confrontation* (New York: St. Martin's Press, 2007).

42. Trita Parsi, *Treacherous Alliance: The Secret Dealings of Israel, Iran, and the U.S.* (New Haven: Yale University Press, 2008), 243–249.

43. Ronen Bergman, *The Secret War with Iran: The 30-Year Covert Struggle for Control of a Rogue State* (Oxford: Oneworld, 2008).

44. Parsi, *Treacherous Alliance*, 4.

45. Laura Rozen, "With Turmoil in Tehran, Obama's Policy in Flux," *Foreign Policy* (June 18, 2009), http://thecable.foreignpolicy.com/posts/2009/06/17/with_turmoil_in_tehran_obama_s_policy_in_flux; Donald MacIntyre, "Israelis May Emigrate over Nuclear Threat," *Independent* (May 23, 2009), http://www.independent.co.uk/news/world/middle-east/israelis-may-emigrate-over-nuclear-threat-1689771.html.

46. Roger Cohen, "What Iran's Jews Say," *New York Times* (February 22, 2009), http://www.nytimes.com/2009/02/23/opinion/23cohen.html?_r=1; U.S Department of State, "2009 Report on International Religious Freedom," in chapter on Iran, Bureau of Democracy, Human Rights and Labor (October 26, 2009), http://www.state.gov/g/drl/rls/irf/2009/127347.htm.

47. Karim Sadjadpour, *Reading Khamenei: The World View of Iran's Most Powerful Leader* (Washington DC: Carnegie Endowment for International Peace, 2008), available at http://www.carnegieendowment.org/files/sadjadpour_iran_final2.pdf; Nazila Fathi, "Iran's President Says Israel Must be 'Wiped off the Map,'" *New York Times* (October 26, 2005), http://www.nytimes.com/2005/10/26/international/middleeast/26cnd-iran.html.

48. Author conversation with former Iranian diplomat, Amman, Jordan, July 2009.

49. Nazila Fathi, 'U.N. Scrutiny Won't Make Iran Quit Nuclear Effort, President Says,' *New York Times* (January 15 2006), http://www.nytimes.com/2006/01/15/international/middleeast/15tehran.html?ex=1294981200&en=aa775eeb6ae97fbd&ei=5088&partner=rssnyt&emc=rss.

50. Ze'ev Schiff, "How Iran Planned the Buenos Aires Blast," *Haaretz*, http://www.haaretz.com/hasen/pages/ShArt.jhtml?itemNo=273898&contrassID=2&subContrassID=1&sbSubContrassID=0.

51. "Iran: Two More Executions for Homosexual Conduct," *Human Rights Watch News* (November 21, 2005), http://www.hrw.org/en/news/2005/11/21/iran-two-more-executions-homosexual-conduct.

52. President George W. Bush's Speech at the Knesset (May 15, 2008), http://www.pmo.gov.il/NR/exeres/99A8266D-3A74–4CCF-BECF-80586554ACBC,frameless.htm?NRMODE=Published.

Chapter 2

1. "60 Years After: Auschwitz/Birkenau Flyover," Israeli Air Force (September 4, 2003), http://www.iaf.org.il/Templates/Flight-Log/FlightLog.aspx?lang=EN&lobbyID=40&folderID=48&subfolderID=325&docfolderID=397&docID=21568&docType=EVENT; see also Amiram Barkat, "IAF Pilots Conduct Fly-Over at Auschwitz Death Camp," *Haaretz*, (September 5, 2003), http://www.haaretz.com/hasen/pages/ShArt.jhtml?itemNo=337012.

2. The presentation of Israeli military options herein originally appeared in Steven Simon, "An Israeli Strike on Iran," *CPA Contingency Planning Memorandum No. 5*, Council on Foreign Relations (November 2009), http://www.cfr.org/publication/20637/israeli_strike_on_iran.html. The analysis drew on Austin Long and Whitney Raas, "Osirak Redux? Assessing Israeli Capabilities to Destroy Iranian Nuclear Facilities," *International Security* 31, no. 4 (Spring 2007): 7–33; and Anthony Cordesman and Abdullah Toukan, "Study on a Possible Israeli Strike on Iran's Nuclear Development Facilities," *Center for Strategic and International Studies* (March 14, 2009), http://csis.org/files/media/csis/pubs/090316_israelistrikeiran.pdf. Additional information is also available in Kenneth M. Pollack, Daniel L. Byman, Martin S. Indyk, Suzanne Maloney, and Michael E. O'Hanlon, *Which Path to Persia? Options for a New American Strategy toward Iran* (Washington D.C.: Brookings Institution Press, 2009).

3. Authors' meeting with Shlomo Brom, Tel Aviv, July 2009.

4. Israeli Prime Minister Benjamin Netanyahu's Speech at the UN General Assembly (September 24, 2009), http://www.pmo.gov.il/PMOEng/Communication/PMSpeaks/speechUN240909.htm.

5. Authors' meeting with Ariel Levite, Tel Aviv, July 2009.

6. Jeffrey Goldberg, "Israel's Fears, Amalek's Arsenal," *New York Times* (May 16, 2009), http://www.nytimes.com/2009/05/17/opinion/17goldberg.html?_r=1&pagewanted=1.

7. Richard K. Betts, "The Osirak Fallacy," *National Interest* (Spring 2006), http://www.columbia.edu/cu/siwps/images/newsletter3/Betts%20-%20Osirak%20Fallacy.pdf.

8. Admiral Mike Mullen, chairman of the Joint Chiefs of Staff, on "Face the Nation," *CBS News* (July 5, 2009), http://www.cbsnews.com/blogs/2009/07/05/politics/politicalhotsheet/entry5134362.shtml, and Re-marks by U.S. Secretary of Defense Robert Gates at a meeting of the Economic Club of Chicago (July 16, 2009), http://www.defense.gov/transcripts/transcript.aspx?transcriptid=4445.

9. "Remarks by President Obama and Prime Minister Netanyahu of Israel" (May 18, 2009), http://www.whitehouse.gov/the_press_office/Remarks-by-President-Obama-and-Israeli-Prime-Minister-Netanyahu-in-press-availability/.

10. As a visitor to the White House, however, Netanyahu was boxed in by Obama's framing of the issue and by the context; the Israeli prime minister, in his first official encounter with a popular president in the first year of his administration, was not in a position to contradict his host. His response took the form of an adroit retreat that sidestepped Obama's assertion of linkage—indeed, turned it upside down: "There isn't a policy linkage and that's what I hear the President saying, and what I'm saying too. And I've always said there's not a policy linkage between pursuing simultaneously peace between Israel and the Palestinians and the rest of the Arab world, and to trying to deal with removing the threat of a nuclear bomb." Ibid.

11. Matt Levitt, "Hezbollah Finances: Funding the Party of God," in Jeanne K. Giraldo and Harold A. Trinkunas (eds.), *Terrorism Financing and State Responses: A Comparative Perspective* (Stanford University Press, 2007), pp. 134–151; Daniel Byman, *Deadly Connections: States that Sponsor Terrorism* (Cambridge University Press, 2005).

12. *Country Reports on Terrorism 2008, Chapter 3: State Sponsors of Terrorism*, U.S. Department of State, Office of the Coordinator for Counterterrorism, http://www.state.gov/s/ct/rls/crt/2008/122436.htm. See also C. I. Bosley, "Iran Allegedly Skirts Hezbollah Arms Ban," *Arms Control Today* 37, no. 7 (September 2007), http://www.armscontrol.org/print/2720; "Egyptian Paper: Iranian Arms Ship

Bound for Gaza Destroyed Off Sudan," *Haaretz* (April 28, 2009), http://www.haaretz.com/hasen/spages/1081382.html; "U.S. Navy Stopped Iran Ship Carrying Weapons and Headed to Gaza," *World Tribune* (January 23, 2009), http://www.worldtribune.com/worldtribune/WTARC/2009/me_iran0069_01_23.asp; C. I. Bosley, "Iran Allegedly Skirts Hezbollah Arms Ban," *Arms Control Association* (September 2007), http://www.armscontrol.org/print/2720; "Turkey Seizes 'Iranian' Weapons," *Al Jazeera* (May 31, 2007), http://english.aljazeera.net/news/europe/2007/05/2008525143259430498.html.

13. Author interview with Georgetown University Professor Daniel Byman. On Hamas's falling popularity, see "Poll Finds Support for Hamas Dropping, Most Support Elections," *Ma'an News Agency* (November 5, 2009), http://www.maannews.net/eng/ViewDetails.aspx?ID=237358; Lourdes Garcia-Navarro, "In Gaza, Hamas Finds Popularity Waning," *NPR* (October 27, 2009), http://www.npr.org/templates/story/story.php?storyId=114208630.

14. "Jones: Middle East Peace 'Epicenter' of Policy," *JTA* (October 28, 2009), http://www.jta.org/news/article/2009/10/28/1008782/jones-middle-east-peace-epicenter-of-policy.

15. Author interview with Aaron D. Miller, a career State Department official who served at the time as an adviser on Middle East issues to Secretary of State James Baker.

16. F. Gregory Gause III, *The International Relations of the Persian Gulf* (Cambridge: Cambridge University Press, 2009), 243.

17. Interview with former U.S. ambassador to Saudi Arabia, Chas Freeman, http://www.pbs.org/wgbh/pages/frontline/shows/saud/etc/script.html.

18. Henry Kissinger, *Diplomacy* (New York: Simon and Schuster, 1994), 719.

19. Authors' meeting with David Menashri, July 2009, Tel Aviv.

20. Author's telephone interview with Ray Takeyh, February 2010.

21. Author interview with Nigel Inkster, former assistant chief and director for operations and intelligence of the British Secret Intelligence Service (SIS), London, March 2010.

22. Matthew Yglesias, "Dueling Headlines" (March 3, 2009), http://yglesias.thinkprogress.org/archives/2009/03/dueling_headlines_2.php.

23. Ethan Bronner, "Israel Reminds Foes That It Has Teeth," *New York Times* (December 28, 2008), http://www.nytimes.com/2008/12/29/world/middleeast/29assess.html.

24. Prime Minister Ehud Olmert told Haaretz in an interview, November 28, 2007, following the Annapolis conference: "Olmert to Haaretz: Two-State Solution, or Israel Is Done For," *Haaretz* (November 29, 2007), http://www.haaretz.com/hasen/spages/929439.html.

25. Rory McCarthy, "Barack: Make Peace with Palestinians or Face Apartheid," guardian.co.uk (February 3, 2010), http://www.guardian.co.uk/world/2010/feb/03/barak-apartheid-palestine-peace.

26. Eugene Rogan and Avi Shlaim (eds.), *The War for Palestine* (Cambridge: Cambridge University Press 2007).

27. "The issue today is not the Gulf of Aqaba or the Strait of Tiran or U.N.E.F. The issue is the rights of the people of Palestine, the aggression against Palestine that took place in 1948, with the help of Britain and the United States....They want to confine it to the straits of Tiran, U.N.E.F. and the rights of passage. We want the rights of the people of Palestine—complete." Nasser speech to Egyptian National Assembly, May 29, 1967, cited in O'Brien, *The Siege*, (London: Paladin 1988) 413.

28. For example, Palestinian negotiator Saeb Erekat has warned that the window for a two-state solution is closing; see Akiva Eldar, "Palestinians Threaten to Adopt One-State Solution," *Haaretz* (February 26, 2010), http://www.haaretz.com/hasen/spages/1152493.html.

29. Aluf Benn, "Better occupation than partial peace," *Haaretz* (October 3, 2008), http://www.haaretz.com/hasen/spages/1024213.html.

30. Joint Palestinian-Israeli Public Opinion Poll, Harry S. Truman Research Institute for the Advancement of Peace at the Hebrew University of Jerusalem and the Palestinian Center for Policy and Survey Research in Ramallah (September 10–19, 2006), http://www.cfr.org/publication/11516/;
Joint Israeli-Palestinian Poll, Truman Institute and Palestinian Center (May 21–June 3, 2009), http://www.pcpsr.org/survey/polls/2009/p32ejoint.html.

31. Quartet Roadmap to Israeli-Palestinian Peace (April 30, 2003), http://www.mideastweb.org/quartetrm3.htm.

32. Mark A. Heller, "Israel's Dilemmas," *Survival* 42, no. 4 (Winter 2000): 21–34.

33. Hussein Agha and Robert Malley, "Camp David: The Tragedy of Errors," *New York Review of Books* 48, no. 13 (August 9, 2001), http://www.nybooks.com/articles/14380; Ron Pundak, "From Oslo to Taba: What Went Wrong?" *Survival* 43, no. 3 (Autumn 2001): 31–45.

34. Prime Minister Netanyahu foreign policy address at Bar-Ilan University (June 14, 2009), http://www.mfa.gov.il/MFA/Government/Speeches+by+Israeli+leaders/2009/Address_PM_Netanyahu_Bar-Ilan_University_14-Jun-2009.htm.

35. Hussein Agha and Robert Malley, "Israel and Palestine: Can They Start Over?" *New York Review of Books* 56, no. 19 (December 3, 2009), http://www.nybooks.com/articles/23456; and author's communication with Robert Malley.

36. On the Jordanian option, see Thomas L. Friedman, "Time for Radical Pragmatism," *New York Times* (June 4, 2008) and former Israeli national security advisor Major General (ret.) Giora Eiland, *The Future of the Two State Solution*, Jerusalem Center for Public Affairs, http://www.jcpa.org/JCPA/Templates/ShowPage.asp?DBID=1&LNGID=1&TMID=111&FID=442&PID=0&IID=2865.

37. They point to, among other things, Israel's insistence that any Palestinian state that emerges will have to be demilitarized; see Netenyahu's Bar-Ilan Speech, June 14, 2009.

38. Hussein Agha and Robert Malley, "Israel and Palestine: Can They Start Over?" *New York Review of Books* 56, no. 19 (December 3, 2009), http://www.nybooks.com/articles/23456.

39. Kissinger, *Years of Upheaval* (Boston: Little, Brown, 1982), 460.

Chapter 3

1. Dennis C. Blair, "Annual Threat Assessment of the Intelligence Community for the Senate Select Committee on Intelligence" (February 12 2009), http://intelligence.senate.gov/090212/blair.pdf.

2. Steven Simon and Jonathan Stevenson, "Disarming Hezbollah," *Foreign Affairs* (January 11, 2010), http://www.foreignaffairs.com/articles/65921/steven-simon-and-jonathan-stevenson/disarming-hezbollah.

3. Taghreed El-Khodary and Isabel Kershner, "6 Palestinians Killed in Gaza at Fatah Rally," *New York Times* (November 13, 2007), http://www.nytimes.com/2007/11/13/world/middleeast/13mideast.html.

4. Babak Rahimi, "Iranian Leaders Weigh Support for the Houthi Rebellion in Yemen," *Terrorism Monitor* 7, no. 35 (November 19, 2009).

5. Which merged in 1990 with South Yemen.

6. "Iran Warns Regional Powers against Intervention in Yemen: Saudi to Bomb Rebels until They Retreat: Minister," *Al Arabiya* (November 10, 2009), http://www.alarabiya.net/articles/2009/11/10/90803.html.

7. "Iran: The Crescent of Crisis," *Time* (January 15, 1979), http://www.time.com/time/magazine/article/0,9171,919995-1,00.html.

8. Michael Slackman and Hassan M. Fattah, "In Public View, Saudis Counter Iran in Region," *New York Times* (February 6, 2007), http://www.nytimes.com/2007/02/06/world/middleeast/06saudi.html?_r=1.

9. Emile Nakhleh, *A Necessary Engagement: Reinventing America's Relations with the Muslim World* (Princeton, N.J.: Princeton University Press, 2009), 27–29.

10. Tariq Al-Homayed, "His Majesty King Abdullah II Interview with Asharq Al Awsat," *Asharq Al Awsat* (January 23, 2007), http://www.jordanembassyus.org/hmka01232007.htm.

11. J. J. Goldberg, "Egypt's Escalating War on Hezbollah," *Forward* (April 24, 2009), http://www.forward.com/articles/104854/.

12. Aziz El-Kaissouni and Will Rasmussen, "Egypt State-Controlled Paper Denounces Hezbollah," *Reuters* (April 21, 2009), http://www.reuters.com/article/idUSTRE53B16G20090412.

13. Danny Ayalon, "Danny Ayalon Pens Historic Op-Ed in Largest Pan-Arab Daily Newspaper," *Asharq Alawsat* (December 15,

2009), http://www.mfa.gov.il/MFA/About+the+Ministry/Deputy_ Foreign_Minister/Speeches/DepFM_Ayalon_Asharq_Alawsat_op- ed_15-Dec-2009.htm; for the original text see http://www.aawsat. com/leader.asp?section=3&article=548663&issueno=11340.

14. David S. Cloud, "U.S. Set to Offer Huge Arms Deal to Saudi Arabia," *New York Times* (July 28, 2007), http://www.nytimes. com/2007/07/28/washington/28weapons.html?_r=1.

15. Thom Shanker, "Despite Slump, U.S. Role as Top Arms Supplier Grows," *New York Times* (September 6, 2009). These figures are drawn from a CRS study, which uses figures in 2008 dollars, adjusted for inflation.

16. Adam Entous and Doina Chiacu, "U.S. Expanding Missile Defenses in the Gulf," *Reuters* (January 31, 2010), http://www.reuters.com/article/idUSTRE60U18R20100131.

17. General David Petraeus, Fifth Plenary Session, *The Manama Dialogue,* Manama, Bahrain (December 12, 2009), http://www.iiss. org/conferences/the-iiss-regional-security-summit/manama-dialogue-2009/plenary-sessions-and-speeches-2009/fifth-plenary-session/question-and-answer-session/.

18. Assuming that they had the necessary aircraft on alert and time to respond—conditions that Jordanian, Syrian and Kuwaiti air forces could probably not meet.

19. David Pollock, "Saudi Public Backs Iran Sanctions but split on Military Action," *Real Clear World* (January 13, 2010), http://www. realclearworld.com/articles/2010/01/13/saudi_public_backs_iran_ sanctions_but_split_on_military_action_97479.html.

20. Isabel Kershner, "Israeli Minister Adds Heat to Exchange with Syria," *New York Times* (February 4, 2010), http://www.nytimes. com/2010/02/05/world/middleeast/05mideast.html.

Chapter 4

1. International Institute for Strategic Studies, *The Military Balance 2010,* vol. 110 (London: Routledge, 2010), 255; Anthony H. Cordesman, "Israeli Weapons of Mass Destruction," *Center for Stra-*

tegic and International Studies (June 2, 2008), http://csis.org/files/media/csis/pubs/080602_israeliwmd.pdf.

2. Gamal Essam El-Din, "No Need for Nukes," *Al-Ahram Weekly*, no. 977 (December 17–23, 2009), http://weekly.ahram.org.eg/2009/977/fr1.htm.

3. Lakhdar Brahimi comments at IISS workshop in Cairo, January 2009.

4. "Egypt: The Usual Suspect" in *Nuclear Programmes in the Middle East: In the Shadow of Iran,* IISS Strategic Dossier (London: IISS, May 20, 2008), p. 29.

5. Borzou Daragahi, "U.S., UAE Reach Nuclear Agreement," *LA Times* (December 16, 2008), http://articles.latimes.com/2008/dec/16/world/fg-gulfnukes16.

6. Remarks by President Obama, Prague (April 5. 2009), http://www.whitehouse.gov/the_press_office/Remarks-By-President-Barack-Obama-In-Prague-As-Delivered/.

7. Richard Perle, for example, later told a television interviewer, "I don't think Ronald Reagan has ever been comfortable with nuclear weapons. And this idea of a nuclear-free world, which I think is rubbish, and dangerous rubbish, has always been present in his thinking. But it wasn't always obvious to his supporters." Dana H. Allin, *Cold War Illusions: America, Europe and Soviet Power, 1969–1989* (New York: St. Martin's Press, 1994), 99.

8. See George P. Schultz, William J. Perry, Henry A. Kissinger, and Sam Nunn, "A World Free of Nuclear Weapons," *Wall Street Journal* (January 4, 2007), http://www.fcnl.org/issues/item_print.php?item_id=2252&issue_id=54, and George P. Schultz, William J. Perry, Henry A. Kissinger, and Sam Nunn, "Toward a Nuclear-Free World," *Wall Street Journal* (January 15, 2008), http://online.wsj.com/public/article_print/SB120036422673589947.html.

9. They also question the realist assumption that only the threat of nuclear annihilation can deter nuclear aggression.

10. Parsi, *Treacherous Alliance*, 248.

11. "Bucharest Summit Declaration," issued by the heads of state and government participating in the meeting of the North

Atlantic Council, Bucharest (April 3, 2008), http://www.nato.int/cps/en/natolive/official_texts_8443.htm.

12. An argument made forcefully by Russian analyst Alexei Arbatov at the 7th IISS Global Strategic Review, Geneva (September 12, 2009), http://www.iiss.org/conferences/global-strategic-review/global-strategic-review-2009/plenary-sessions-and-speeches-2009/third-plenary-session-alexi-arbatov/.

13. Author interviews with State Department officials, Vienna, Austria, and Washington D.C., during the course of 2009.

14. Mark Fitzpatrick, "A Prudent Decision on Missile Defence," *Survival* 51, no. 6 (December 2009–January 2010): 8.

15. Author interview with Obama administration official, November 2009.

16. "Medvedev Signals Openness to Iran Sanctions after Talks," *CNN* (September 24, 2009), http://edition.cnn.com/2009/POLITICS/09/23/us.russia.iran/.

17. Russia has significant trade and technological relations with Iran, including its nuclear reactor at Bushehr. Bilateral trade between the two countries was estimated at over $3 billion in 2007. Russia has also undertaken to sell advanced SS-300 air defense missiles to Iran, but given the fact that their delivery would probably have precipitated an Israeli attack, the deal has been postponed indefinitely.

18. Mark Landler, "Clinton Raises U.S. Concerns of Military Power in Iran," *New York Times* (February 16, 2010), http://www.nytimes.com/2010/02/16/world/middleeast/16diplo.html.

19. Http://www.roozonline.com/english/news/newsitem/article/2009/march/28//waiting-for-actual-changes.html; video of response (with English subtitles) at http://videotube.ronaky.com/video/t_0AHcsYqIs/iranian-supreme-leader-ayatollah-khamenei-responds-to-us-president-obamas-nowruz-message.html.

20. Rami Khouri, "Why Chuckles Greeted Hillary's Gulf Tour," *Daily Star* (February 17, 2010), http://www.dailystar.com.lb/article.asp?edition_id=10&categ_id=5&article_id=111835#axzz0qBjoI5b4.

21. Richard N. Haass, "Enough Is Enough," *Newsweek* (January 22, 2010), http://www.newsweek.com/id/231991.

22. The leading reformist presidential candidate, Mir Hossein Mousavi, for example, opposed it: "The discussions in Geneva were

really surprising, and if the promises given [to the West] are realized, then the hard work of thousands of scientists would be ruined....And if we cannot keep our promises then it would prepare the ground for harder sanctions against the country." http://www.washingtonpost. com/wp-dyn/content/article/2009/10/29/AR2009102900418.html.

23. Mark Fitzpatrick, "Can Iran's Nuclear Capability Be Kept Latent?" *Survival* 49, no. 1 (Spring 2007): 49.

24. President Nicolas Sarkozy at the Security Council Summit on Nuclear Non-Proliferation and Disarmament (September 24, 2009), http://www.franceonu.org/spip.php?article4170.

25. Author discussion with Martin Briens, London, February 2010.

26. William J. Broad, "Iran President Says Nuclear Enrichment Will Grow," *New York Times* (December 2, 2009), http://www. nytimes.com/2009/12/03/world/middleeast/03nuke.html.

27. David E. Sanger and William J. Broad, "U.S. Sees and Opportunity to Press Iran on Nuclear Fuel," *New York Times* (January 3, 2010), http://www.nytimes.com/2010/01/03/world/middleeast/03iran. html.

Chapter 5

1. Julie Bosman, "Clinton Turns from Anger to Sarcasm" (February 24, 2008), http://thecaucus.blogs.nytimes.com/2008/02/24/clinton-turns-from-anger-to-sarcasm/.

2. Patrick Healy and Abby Goodnough, "Clinton and Obama Intensify Attacks," *New York Times* (March 2, 2008), http://www. nytimes.com/2008/03/02/us/politics/02campaign.html?fta=y.

3. "In Their Own Words: Obama on Reagan," *New York Times*, http://www.nytimes.com/ref/us/politics/21seelye-text.html.

4. Barack Obama, *The Audacity of Hope* (New York: Crown, 2006), 31–32, 289.

5. Dana H. Allin, *Cold War Illusions: America, Europe and Soviet Power, 1969–1989* (New York: St. Martin's Press, 1994), 77 passim.

6. Hendrik Hertzberg, "The Child Monarch," *New Republic* 205, no.11 (September 9, 1991): 34.

7. Hendrik Hertzberg, "Election Day," *New Yorker* (November 2008), http://www.newyorker.com/online/blogs/hendrikhertzberg/2008/11/2.html.

8. Robert Dallek, *An Unfinished Life: John F. Kennedy 1917–1963* (New York: Back Bay Books, 2004), 708.

9. John F. Kennedy, Inaugural Address, Washington D.C., January 20, 1961, http://www.jfklibrary.org/Historical+Resources/Archives/Reference+Desk/Speeches/JFK/003POF03Inaugural01201961.htm.

10. Dallek, *Unfinished Life*, 619.

11. National Security Council, *The National Security Strategy* (September 2002), 15, http://georgewbush-whitehouse.archives.gov/nsc/nss/2002/; see also, Edward Rhodes, "The Imperial Logic of Bush's Liberal Agenda," *Survival* 45, no. 1 (Spring 2003): 135.

12. National Security Council, *National Security Strategy*, ii.

13. "Rice Calls for Mid-East Democracy," *BBC News* (June 20, 2005), http://news.bbc.co.uk/1/hi/4109902.stm.

14. Marc Lynch, "Arab Public Opinion in 2009," *Foreign Policy* (May 20, 2009), http://lynch.foreignpolicy.com/posts/2009/05/19/arab_public_opinion_in_2009; "The 2009 Arab Public Opinion Poll: A View from the Middle East," Brookings Institution, Washington D.C. (May 19, 2009), http://www.brookings.edu/~/media/Files/events/2009/0519_arab_opinion/20090519_poll.pdf; "2009 Annual Arab Public Opinion Survey," University of Maryland with Zogby International (April–May 2009), http://www.brookings.edu/~/media/Files/events/2009/0519_arab_opinion/2009_arab_public_opinion_poll.pdf.

15. Fouad Ajami, "The Obama Spell Is Broken," *Wall Street Journal* (February 2, 2010), http://online.wsj.com/article/SB10001424052748704094304575029110104772360.html?mod=WSJ_hpp_sections_opinion; Eliot A. Cohen, "Taking the Measure of Obama's Foreign Policy," *Wall Street Journal* (February 11, 2010), http://online.wsj.com/article/SB10001424052748703481004574646080636258614.html.

16. Michael Levenson and Jonathan Saltzman, "At Harvard Law, a Unifying Voice: Classmates Recall Obama as Even-Handed Leader," *Boston Globe* (January 28, 2007), http://www.boston.com/news/local/articles/2007/01/28/at_harvard_law_a_unifying_voice/; "Obama at

House Republican Retreat in Baltimore: Full Video, Text," *Huffington Post* (January 29, 2010), http://www.huffingtonpost.com/2010/01/29/transcript-of-president-o_n_442423.html.

17. "Remarks by the President on a New Beginning," Cairo University, Cairo, Egypt (June 4, 2009), http://www.whitehouse.gov/the_press_office/Remarks-by-the-President-at-Cairo-University-6-04-09/.

18. John F. Kennedy, American University Commencement Address (June 10, 1963), http://usa.usembassy.de/etexts/speeches/rhetoric/jfkuniv.htm.

19. Ryan Lizza, "Battle Plans: How Obama Won," *New Yorker* (November 17, 2008), http://www.newyorker.com/reporting/2008/11/17/081117fa_fact_lizza.

20. Allin, *Cold War Illusions*, passim and especially chapter 7; Timothy Garton Ash, *In Europe's Name: Germany and the Divided Continent* (London: Jonathan Cape, 1993), 257–258.

21. To be sure, economic issues were more salient—with pocketbook concerns more important to voters than the fate of the Palestinians or Islamist prospects in Lebanon.

22. Author conversation with Bernard Hourcade, July 2009.

23. Interview with Professor David Menashri on Iran's elections: "Fighting within the family," *Israel Policy Forum*, http://www.israelpolicyforum.org/blog/interview-prof-david-menashri-iran-s-elections-fighting-within-family.

24. Nader Mousavizadeh, "The Bystander: Obama Grapples with the Revolution," *New Republic* (July 15, 2009), http://www.tnr.com/article/the-bystander.

25. "The Islamic Republic at 31," Human Rights Watch (February 11, 2010), http://www.hrw.org/en/reports/2010/02/11/islamic-republic-31.

26. "Statement from the President on Iran" (June 20, 2009), http://www.whitehouse.gov/the_press_office/statement-from-the-president-on-iran/.

27. David Brooks, "The Chicago View," *New York Times* (June 5, 2009), http://www.nytimes.com/2009/06/05/opinion/05brooks.html.

28. Laura Rozen, "In Letters, Obama Asked Arab States for Confidence-Building Measures toward Israel," *Foreign Policy* (July 26, 2009), http://thecable.foreignpolicy.com/posts/2009/07/26/in_letters_obama_asks_arab_states_for_confidence_building_measures_towards_israel.

29. "Saudi Rebuffs US Pleas for Peace Gestures toward Israel," *Daily Star* (August 1, 2009), http://www.thedailystar.net/newDesign/latest_news.php?nid=18389; "Jordan Rejects US Call to Improve Ties with Israel," *MSNBC News* (August 3, 2009), http://abcnews.go.com/Politics/wireStory?id=8240256.

30. Michael Slackman, "Arab States Cool to Obama Pleas for Peace Gesture," *New York Times* (June 2, 2009), http://www.nytimes.com/2009/06/03/world/middleeast/03saudi.html?_r=1&scp=14&sq=obama%20saudi%20king%20visit&st=cse.

31. Obama at this point seems to have decided to follow through on the idea of bringing Dennis Ross to the White House, where it was thought that his long experience and political savvy would obviate the sorts of the diplomatic fiascos that marked his first six months in office. Laura Rozen, "Revisiting Obama's Riyadh Meeting" (July 17, 2009), http://thecable.foreignpolicy.com/posts/2009/07/17/revisiting_obamas_riyadh_meeting.

32. Mark Landler and Isabel Kershner, "Israeli Settlement Growth Must Stop, Clinton Says," *New York Times* (May 27, 2009), http://www.nytimes.com/2009/05/28/world/middleeast/28mideast.html.

33. Interview by Ali El-Saleh and Nazer Majli, "A Conversation with President Mahmud Abbas," *Asharq al Awsat* (March 4, 2010), http://www.asharq-e.com/news.asp?section=3&id=19247.

34. Robert Burns, "Clinton Calls Israeli Concessions 'Unprecedented,' *AP Jerusalem* (October 31, 2009), http://abcnews.go.com/International/wireStory?id=8963297.

35. Author interview with high-ranking State Department official, Washington, D.C., November 2009.

36. See, for example, Aaron D Miller, *The Much Too Promised Land: America's Elusive Search for Arab-Israeli Peace* (New York: Bantam Dell 2008), 94–102

37. See http://thecable.foreignpolicy.com/posts/2009/05/28/netanyahu_what_the_hell_do_they_want_with_me.

38. M. J. Rosenberg, "If Health Reform Fails, Netanyahu Will Prevail on Settlements," *TPM Cafe Blog* (July 24, 2009), http://tpmcafe.talkingpointsmemo.com/2009/07/24/the_nexus_between_health_care_and_west_bank_settle/; Steven Karatt, "What Netanyahu Knows about Obama Healthcare," *Jewish National Initiative*, http://www.jni.co.il/rec/107-What-Netanyahu-Knows-About-Obama-Healthcare.

39. J. J. Goldberg, "On Obama and Israel, Rage without Reason—Good Fences," *Forward—The Jewish Daily* (July 29, 2009), http://www.forward.com/articles/111011/.

40. See Jeffrey Goldberg, "The White House Reacts to Aluf Benn's Arguments" *Atlantic* (July 28, 2009), http://jeffreygoldberg.theatlantic.com/archives/2009/07/the_white_house_reacts_to_aluf.php.

41. Matthew Kalman/Har Bracha, "Huckabee's First 2012 Campaign Stop: Israel," *Time* (August 19, 2009), http://www.time.com/time/politics/article/0,8599,1917389,00.html; Alan B. Goldberg and Katie N. Thomson, "Sarah Palin on Bristol Pregnancy: 'I Was Shocked': In Wide-Ranging Interview, Palin Opens Up to Barbara Walters on Private Life, Presidential Ambitions" (November 13, 2009), http://abcnews.go.com/Politics/sarah-palin-speaks-barbara-walters/story?id=9077549.

42. John Lloyd, "Rowing Alone," *Financial Times* (August 3, 2002).

43. Mark Landler and Ethan Bronner, "Israel Feeling Rising Anger from the U.S.," *New York Times* (March 15, 2010), http://www.nytimes.com/2010/03/16/world/middleeast/16mideast.html?hp.

44. The *New York Times*'s Roger Cohen explained well why the Netanyahu excuse, that "Jerusalem is not a settlement," was a "cheap" evasion. "I say cheap because everyone knows Jerusalem is not a settlement. That's not the issue. The issue is that the Israeli annexation of East Jerusalem is rejected by the rest of the world and any peace agreement will involve an inventive deal on its status. To build is therefore to provoke." Roger Cohen, 'Lo, the Mideast Moves' *New York Times* (March 29 2010), http://www.nytimes.com/2010/03/30/opinion/30iht-edcohen.html.

45. Aluf Benn, "Why Won't Obama Talk to Israel?" *New York Times* (July 27, 2009), http://www.nytimes.com/2009/07/28/opinion/28benn.html.

46. David E. Sanger and Eric Schmitt, "U.S. Speeding Up Missile Defenses in Persian Gulf," *New York Times* (January 30 2010), http://www.nytimes.com/2010/01/31/world/middleeast/31missile.html?hp.

47. Authors' interview with James Dobbins, Washington, D.C., July 2009.

48. See "Obama's Address on the War in Afghanistan," *New York Times* (December 1, 2009), http://www.nytimes.com/2009/12/02/world/asia/02prexy.text.html.

49. Jeffrey Goldberg, "The Four Questions: Martin Indyk on the Failure of Peacemaking," *Atlantic* (January 27, 2009), http://www.theatlantic.com/personal/archive/2009/01/the-four-questions-martin-indyk-on-the-failure-of-peacemaking/9441/.

50. For a U.S. army CENTCOM assessment of the effects on America's strategic interests, see "Statement of General David H. Petraeus, U.S. Army Commander U.S. Central Command before the Senate Armed Services Committee (March 16, 2010), http://armedservices.senate.gov/statemnt/2010/03 % 20March/Petraeus % 20 03–16–10.pdf.

51. "X" (George F. Kennan), "The Sources of Soviet Conduct," *Foreign Affairs* (July 1947), http://www.foreignaffairs.com/articles/23331/x/the-sources-of-soviet-conduct.

52. Freedman, *Choice of Enemies*, 69, 72.

Index